Foreword by John Bevere

ACCEPTED.
MY JOURNEY

Dean Sikes

FOREWORD BY JOHN BEVERE

ACCEPTED

MY JOURNEY

DEAN SIKES

ISBN # 978-1-7923-5563-9

POST OFFICE BOX 8915

CHATTANOOGA, TENNESSEE 37414

WWW.DEANSIKES.NET

"… He made us **_ACCEPTED_** in the Beloved."

Ephesians 1:6 (NKJV)

6

For My Wife, Lori

From the first day we met in July of 1995, you *accepted* me. Your commitment to the Lord, to our family, and the love with which you love me gave me the courage to write this book.

You've taught me how to give and to receive love and for this I will always be grateful.

I love you, Lu, with all of my HEART.

TABLE OF CONTENTS

PART FOUR: THE ACCEPTANCE

PART FIVE: THE APPLICATION TO YOUR LIFE

PART ONE

INTRODUCTION

FOREWORD

At the core of our being, we all desire to be accepted. From early on, we seek this acceptance from family and friends; then as our world enlarged, we sought it from others. As we grew, so did our need to be accepted. Unknowingly, we learned to derive our value and worth from the approval of others.

In our search for acceptance, we've often encountered rejection— that horrible feeling that you don't quite measure up, that you've fallen short, and that who you are and what you do is not enough. Whether it's being excluded from a particular event, being overlooked for a promotion at work, or being abandoned by a loved one—we've all faced rejection, and its painful!

When the effects of rejection are left unaddressed, we'll find ourselves trying to sooth the sting by conforming to others—being someone we're not and doing things that are uncharacteristic—all for the sake of acceptance!

At the root of this desire is approval addiction. But there is hope and healing! You can break this cycle and experience freedom.

That's why I'm thrilled that my friend, Dean Sikes, has written *Accepted*. Throughout the pages of this book, Dean uses both the Word of God and personal experiences to help redirect you to the loving embrace of your heavenly Father, where you'll find acceptance, healing, and a love indescribable and that surpasses all understanding! When you've experienced this love for yourself, you'll find what your heart has longed for all along . . . and you'll cease seeking acceptance from others!

JOHN BEVERE

Best-selling Author and Minister

Co-founder of Messenger International

ENDORSEMENTS

Jesus said to the man He had just delivered from a legion of unclean spirits, "Go home to your friends, and tell them [or testify to] what great things The LORD has done for you" (Mark 5:19, *NKJV*).

This book is Dean's personal testimony of what God has done for him "through some very painful portions of my life...that heretofore have never been publicly shared."

Read it, and live it with Dean. God will change your life!

KENNETH COPELAND

When I was given the manuscript for "Accepted" I was not remotely prepared for the journey it took me on. Instead of a "normal" Christian book, it was a real page turner; transparent, vivid in descriptions, and with profound life lessons. My overwhelming impression was how, and who, God calls and equips. You will deeply understand the age-old truth that God loves to use broken vessels. He sees your glorious end even in the toughest of beginnings! It is not our brilliant performances or difficult hardships that matter. As with Dean, we become a fountain of healing to others through dependency on God and His Word, regardless of our history. And so, it can be with you. Do you feel in any way disqualified to be mightily used by God? "Accepted" may be exactly what you need.

ROBERT MURPHREE
Filmmaker

Skiptvet, Norway

I highly recommend *Accepted* by Dean Sikes. What a phenomenal book—it's riveting, it's raw, and it's honest. It goes to the very heart of subjects that people *need* to talk about but so often don't out of misled feelings of guilt, fear, or shame.

Dean really hit a homerun with this book. Yet, in order to do so, he had to open himself up in ways he probably never wanted to. He had to say things he didn't want to say. He had to reveal things about himself, his family, and his relationships that he didn't want to reveal. But he did so because he loves and trusts God and because you're worth it!

I believe this book will not only heal your heart but should also be preached in every church. You'll come to really understand how much you matter and how much you are accepted by God. You'll come away knowing that because of what Jesus has already done for you, you are more than enough!

DR. JESSE DUPLANTIS

President and Founder

Jesse Duplantis Ministries

In *Accepted*, Dean Sikes transparently pours out his heart about serious challenges he has experienced and overcome in life. Very few are willing to be as honest as Dean has been in this book, but because he is willing to lay it all on the line, many readers will be set free. This is not just Dean's story — it is the story of *many* people. But in this book, Dean walks the reader with care into real answers from God's Word — answers that led him to a place of victory and that will lead others there too.

RICK RENNER
Author, Teacher, Pastor, Broadcaster
Moscow, Russia

How amazing it is to read about a man who is so transparent, he is willing to lay down his life's story and not pull any punches.

In "Accepted," Dean Sikes reveals the good, the bad and the ugly in order for us to see the journey he has experienced.

This, "no holds barred" book reveals the struggle of not being accepted — a condition that many of us have faced.

Thank you, Dean for baring your soul and helping us to see our way to our loving, Heavenly Father who loves us unconditionally.

Thank God, we have been accepted!

PASTOR GEORGE PEARSONS

Senior Pastor, Eagle Mountain International Church

Fort Worth, Texas

When a person experiences the pain of rejection and abuse, they are often launched into a downward spiral of fear, shame, and control— but there is freedom and restoration in Jesus! In Dean Sikes latest book, *Accepted,* Dean reveals his personal journey through the pain of rejection and abuse, to complete restoration in the Father's unconditional love. To anyone who has experienced similar things, I believe Dean's powerful story will start a transformation in your own heart, as you discover that you are not alone. There is healing and wholeness available and waiting for you in the arms of your heavenly Father. Keep reading!

DANIEL KOLENDA

President/CEO Christ for all Nations

This awesome book "*Accepted*" is a life changing book and is a jewel of wisdom you must add to the treasure box. I love how transparent Dean gets for us. So much healing. Every opposition we face in life is just another opportunity to display to those around us that we have promises that can be trusted from a God who cares about every detail of our lives. Dean Sikes truly describes the heartbeat of the Father and points everyone into the direction that heals and restores in Jesus Christ. As I read this my heart was ignited. What a tremendous blessing that we serve the only God who restores, renews and gives us do-overs, no matter what. He loves to use people with the worst past to create the best futures. *Accepted* brings you closer to this understanding. This book will awaken you to all the promises that He has for you. Hope starts here!

REAL TALK KIM

Kimberly Jones

Dean Sikes has been a wonderful friend to me for many years. I've watched him minister in a variety of situations. But, I believe the Lord has taken him to a new level with ACCEPTED. This book is painfully honest, yet full of truth and grace. Dean's testimony will not only break you, it will bless you. And, like me, you will be certain to learn many deeper spiritual truths as you read.

CHARLES BILLINGSLEY

My friend Dean has laid his life down for the cause of Christ and can be seen as one of the warriors in the battle for the hearts of the next generation in our time. His life and ministry proclaim the message of Christ's forgiveness and grace upon each of us, especially upon those hurting and in despair. This book is an expression of the courage he has shown in the battle for the next generation. Courage to allow God to use a broken life and craft something extraordinary from it! Dean's life has touched tens of thousands of children in Africa. He has ministered to those who are in despair and even at life's end, effectively showing them the true hope: Jesus Christ. I believe his message of hope in this well-titled book, "ACCEPTED" will encourage every reader and inspire us all to be brave in sharing our testimonies (Rev 12:11). In the words of Billy Graham: "Courage is contagious. When a brave man takes a stand, the spines of others are often stiffened." Thank you Dean for taking a stand!

JACQUES van BOMMEL
Founder and CEO

Reaching a Generation Group

South Africa

Thank you, Lord; thank you Dean. I highly recommend Dean's book, "Accepted'. Dean walks the reader though life experiences and how they molded him. But more importantly, how God and His Word can break the mold you see yourself in and show you that God loves you and that you matter. How fitting is it that Dean's ministry message is, *YOU MATTER*!

LARRY WINTERS
President and Founder,

Leadership Team Development, Inc

Raleigh, North Carolina

Dean Sikes is thoughtful and passionate. He really "gets it," especially since he walked in the shoes of those he ministers to.

He has a no-nonsense authentic approach in partnering with the Lord to facilitate a hand-off from dark to light, from a self-imposed worthless view to a worthwhile worthy introspection in the young minds of the world. Dean gives practical examples of how to address the generational curse and "not being enough". Young minds can become polluted with experiences that seem to reinforce feelings of inadequacy.

I believe that one of the biggest weapons of the enemy is to torment adolescents with perceived or real traumatic experiences. This creates a loop of memory through the limbic system of a child's brain. These destructive thoughts form negative memories which loop in the subconscious mind and continue to create havoc throughout life if left unchecked. Millions of loops in the subconscious mind colors one's perceptions and creates a departure from the Truth.

"Accepted" facilitates an encounter with "The Truth" leading to the opportunity to drink from living water- a thirst quenching experience with our loving heavenly Father.

This work is a valuable weapon in the armamentarium of every warrior that endeavors to conquer past hurts and negative experiences.

AVERY M. JACKSON III MD FACS FAANS

Neurosurgeon

Author of "The God Prescription: Our Heavenly Father's Plan for Spiritual, Mental, and Physical Health"

Founder and Medical Director of the Michigan Neurosurgical Institute PC and MNI Great Lakes ECHO LLC

Dean shares a personal side of himself in his new book, *ACCEPTED*. He emphasizes the importance of dealing with your emotions in order to overcome pain in your past and walks you through how that process transpired in his own life. This book is valuable to any teenager or adult needing to let go of their past in order to have a brighter future and realize that they are accepted.

CALEB BRIDGES

2020 Graduate of Arizona State University

INTRODUCTION

As you read the words in this book, I hope you'll hear my heart. For me to write what you are now reading, I had to first get alone and spend more time with the Holy Spirit than ever before. I was preparing to do something I knew I was being led to do, something that we believe is the single most important assignment thus far in the life of our ministry.

In all honesty, I never intended, nor for that matter, never really wanted to write this book. My preference was to journal and by doing so, identify and then see the Lord eradicate the pain that had been resident in my heart for so many years. But, as you will see later on, the assignment to write this book was not up to me. He made His will and direction concerning this so clear and did so in a very, very public way. My choice, however, was to **obey** what I was being led to do.

Before I wrote the first words, I prayed. And then set out on a journey of journaling what was so deeply and unintentionally buried in my heart. It then became an excursion in discovering why my heart was so shut down; why I wasn't capable in my own strength of allowing anyone into the deepest recesses of my soul; and why for fifty years I had consistently felt like *I wasn't enough* just being me.

During those first six months of journaling, I wrote like never before, meaning that there was no prescribed order of thought. I would just pray and ask the Holy Spirit to give me the words that would begin the journey of unpacking whatever was in my heart and doing so one bucketfull at a time. As I wrote, the overwhelming majority of what was initially revealed in my heart was a troubling combination of anger and pain, both of which had been birthed to some degree from the relationship I had shared with my mom, a relationship that spanned five decades of our lives. As those fifty-year-old scars began to be torn away and my emotions began to bubble to the top, I began to notice that my life had a common, dominant theme running through it and that theme was an assignment from the enemy that I'll share with you in the pages to come.

As days turned into weeks and then months, I wrote in incomplete sentences, and at other times I wrote run-on sentences that ran on and on and on. It didn't matter, and I didn't care. There was no stylistic reasoning in much of what I wrote. There were days I wrote for hours and other days for only minutes. There were days I didn't even think about writing. Why? Because some days the journey was just too much. Over time, I became acutely aware of what a totally emotionally exhaustive experience this was, but irrespective of my feelings and despite my struggle, the Holy Spirit kept nudging me to continue *emptying* out. And so, I obeyed. I wrote and wrote and wrote.

Initially, I wrestled with feeling somewhat anxious in what I was writing as I was cautiously revealing deeply rooted and some very painful portions of my life, portions that heretofore have never been publicly shared. I did so not in an effort to be hurtful or disrespectful to anyone, but to successfully accomplish the assignment this book has on it. Being totally truthful and transparent and doing so in love was the mandate the Lord gave me. With love in my heart and obedience as a guiding force, I kept writing. And as I did, many, many times as the words were flowing from my heart, tears were flowing down my face.

Where my relationship with my mom was concerned, just like all relationships, it was neither all good nor all bad. And like you and me, mom was neither all good nor was she all bad. She was first and foremost a strong Christian who loved God. She was highly motivated, and earlier in her life she was an entrepreneur who created several very successful businesses. During the final twenty-nine years of her life, she had a Christian-based counseling ministry. That said, like all of us, mom had terrific qualities, but she also had some very broken areas in her own life. It was what these broken areas in her life created for and in me that caused me in part to wrestle with anxiety, as the words that became the story of my life took shape into what you're now reading. In spite of an unrelenting assault on my emotions by the enemy (the devil), I did my best to trust God in this process, remained focused, and kept writing.

A funny thing happens when we let go of our attempts at control and instead pursue with unabashed obedience the assignment the Lord reveals as His will for our life ... when we get ourselves out of the way, surrender, and then just obey, He moves in and leads us in the work that you and I could never fully do on our own.

As I continued journaling, there was a day when this journey of emptying out took a turn. It was a day when *revelation* into the core reason He was leading me to write touched the center of my heart and did so with supreme accuracy. I was suddenly no longer feeling anxious. Instead, I was sitting down with a smile on my face and contentment in my heart, knowing that the words He was giving me to write were healing to my soul and would perhaps one day soon be used by His Spirit *to bring spiritual and emotional healing* to those who might be willing to go on this journey with me.

The revelation He gave me had to do with a spiritual term that will be discussed throughout the time you and I invest with one another. The term? GENERATIONAL CURSES. Maybe some of you are all-too-familiar with generational curses and for others, you may have never even heard of them. Either way, whether you're fully aware of what they are or not, for use in our identifying them in this book, let's keep it simple: a generational curse has been defined as "a negative action, behavior, attitude or addiction that increases in strength from one generation to the next, affecting certain members of that family."

It was during this season of journaling that I began to sense a tailwind blowing at my back. I was moving faster and faster towards a destination that would eventually allow me to come in for a landing along still waters and green pastures – a place of rest that offered solitude and peace; two very special gifts from the Lord that to this moment pass my understanding.

Somewhere during that time of solitude and resting in His peace, I realized that I no longer had to wait until I figured it all out to live life the way God intended; nor do you. Instead, we can choose right here, right now, to embrace the love our Heavenly Father has been offering all along; and with His love profoundly serving as the anchor of our soul, we can then choose to move forward in faith, one step at a time, knowing that for those of us who believe the Word of God and apply it to our everyday living, there is the promise of a life of victory.

And so, with that being said, I invite you to join me as I offer you a glimpse into those first days of journaling that gave birth to what you are now reading. Truthfully, this journey has been ugly, disturbing, messy, painful, and yes, at times, even a little scary. Through it all, though, this journey has been honest and without question, healing.

PART TWO

THE ABANDONMENT

MY JOURNALING EXPERIENCE

Today as I sit down and write, this is my first voyage into the world of journaling in decades. Last time I journaled, I did so as a college freshman in English 101. I didn't enjoy the process then and I'm not too sure about it today. That said, I can't deny that as I sit and just write, my heart is waking up.

As I get alone with my thoughts, I find myself immediately fighting the internal battle of HURRY: hurry to write; hurry to go to edit; and hurry to get these deeply introspective thoughts assembled into book form and then distributed into the public space for people to read. I know that *hurry* is the one thing I cannot do. To drive this point home, I sit here in front of my computer as the falling rain pounds against the windows in my office and sense the gentle touch of the hands of the Creator on my shoulders – the Master's touch that offers me the invitation to go about writing this book in His way and in His timing. A way and a time that obliterates the trap of *hurry*. To do this His way requires a definitive choice on my part, a choice that whispers from my lips to His ears the very same words Jesus spoke to His Father while facing His very own moment of consecration while kneeling in a garden thousands of years ago, "Not my will but Yours."

And with His will being the guiding desire of writing, I take a moment to pause and breathe and then do so again and do so with purpose. I intentionally sit in the silence of my office, fighting the temptation to launch into typing. Instead, I find myself listening as this afternoon thunderstorm blows across the parking lot of our office, much in the same way that my emotions over these past five decades have blown across my heart. Sitting in the solitude of my office with *hurry* purposefully being benched on the sidelines, the Holy Spirit gives me the *green light* to keep on writing. I do so, and with every word that appears on the screen, a swarm of heightened emotions suddenly collide in my mind and heart. Slowing down allows these emotions to surface. It's part of His plan.

24

Initially, I encountered anger mixed with pain. Now, months into writing, the three emotions that are surfacing in this internal war that has been declared on my inner being are sadness, acknowledgement and uncertainty. *Sadness* because this process is stirring the pot of the pain. *Acknowledgement* because to get out of the pain and live in divine healing, I'm led to first acknowledge what happened to me and must also begin to let go of that which should have happened but never did. Recognition is half the battle. And *uncertainty* because I'm not too certain yet what seed was sown that produced the harvest of emotional abandonment and sexual abuse. But this I do know: somewhere in all of my praying, time in the Word, and in all of this processing, Jesus the Healer is right here with me; and where He is, nothing evil can co-exist.

Unlike the previous books that I have written since 1993, in what you are now reading, I'm not offering you a *how-to* guide nor am I presenting you with a proven *formula* for discovering your destiny. Here you're being offered a front row seat to my journey with the Holy Spirit, a journey to the very depths of my heart and core of my soul. This journey, though, isn't singularly for me; no, much more importantly, this journey is for you as well. The principles He's leading me to talk about are all principles from the Word of God. Because they're from the Bible, you can be assured that His Word will do exactly what it says it will do in Isaiah 55:11 – "*...It shall not return to Me void, but it shall accomplish what I please, and it shall prosper in the thing for which I sent it.*"

He inspires me to continue typing. With each passing minute the once blank screen is filling with word after word, sentence after sentence and page after page. With no filter and no hindrance affecting the flow of words, which, by the way, is the prerequisite He's given me for this specific journaling exercise, I find that in addition to the emotions that were described above, I also recognize that for quite some time, I've been feeling completely numb. That's the thing about emotions. They're real, and they command our attention. One-way or another, either willingly or by default, even when we feel numb, we will eventually we give attention to the centerpiece of humanity, the heart.

The more time I invest into journaling, the more I see where I am experiencing days having minimal drive and have been emotionally spent; and then there were times (almost always with my family) that I feel safe and ok. Mostly, though, I have felt so sad and terribly lost. Isolated. Sounds stupid and goes against everything I know to be true relating to the scriptural principle that is described in Job 22:28 (*"You will also declare a thing, and it will be established for you; so light will shine on your ways."*), the principle of *confession brings possession*, but today, to say that I have felt emotionally lost and isolated is exactly what I have been feeling. So very tired. The wounds have been so very deep. What has to happen for me to wake up and live life with joy inexpressible? What's my responsibility in this healing process? Why did all of this happen? Why did it happen to me?

Ever find yourself asking those same questions or ones that are similar in your own life? If you have, then you probably understand maybe better than most other people why those questions could inject such a deep, deep sense of hopelessness into the heart and mind; hopelessness that is driven by the lies of the devil. Lies such as, "You caused this;" "Something is really wrong with you;" "Nobody loves you;" and, "You're not enough." The opposite of a lie, though, is the truth. And truth from the Word of God is what this journey is all about. Let's continue.

As I take time to pensively travel back and honestly look at my life, I come face-to-face with several significant occurrences: the emotional disconnection from my mom; the after effects of my having been sexually abused by someone in our church; the anger that was resident in me for so long; the art I mastered of making life about me; my facing off with a generational curse; and the fear of letting go and wholly trusting God. I hope that you will take time to likewise look at your life as we move forward. Maybe you can identify with some or all of what I just listed; and if you can, stay close, continue reading, and trust Jesus to open your eyes and cause you to see the truth He wants to reveal into your life.

Concerning the relationship with my mom, the singular question that immediately races to the forefront of my mind is this: When she was getting sicker and closer to death, why did she *then* tell me that when I was four years old, she had emotionally abandoned me?

Sure, through the years mom and I had experienced pain; but in my mind, forgiveness had been exchanged between us and while the relationship was certainly far from perfect, surely, we could let go of the past, couldn't we? Especially as mom was facing the undeniable progression toward the end of her life. Looking back, with this question still unanswered and with each passing day I can see where my heart was in a wrestling match with time, and time was running out.

Even in this wrestling match, I really enjoyed the almost daily visits we'd share when I would go to the Assisted Living Facility where she lived the last nine months of her life. Yes, we talked, but mostly it was *surface* talk. But what my dad, my sister Deanna, mom's caretakers, and I all took notice of was the unmistakable way I had of making mom smile and oftentimes laugh. She loved when I took her on fast rides in her wheelchair up and down the hallways of the Assisted Living building. Something about the exhilaration that came with our picking up momentum as we headed toward her room, oftentimes on one wheel, that caused her to let go of the control and just joyfully embrace the moment.

But even with the smiles and laughter we shared, I still wondered why mom had told me that she had emotionally abandoned me, and the other looming and unanswered question that for so many years I so desperately wanted to ask but never mustered the courage to do so was, "Why was I *not good enough?*" In light of those questions lingering in an unanswered and unresolved state, maybe you find yourself wondering why I never asked them. As I've considered any number of internal responses to those recurring questions, I've come to realize that I never asked, because I did not want to hear the answer. Subconsciously, I reasoned that as long as I never heard an answer to the *elephant* in the room, I could somehow process the pain and move forward in life in my way and in my own time. That reasoning would prove to be a mistake.

Sitting here now with all of these questions pelting my mind like raindrops pelting against the windows, the Holy Spirit reminds me over-and-over of some timely, godly counsel Pastor George Pearsons has given me. (Pastor George and Terri Pearsons are dear friends, and their influence on our life and ministry are something we cherish.) When mom's and my relationship would hit a rough patch, I would sometimes call Pastor George; and after graciously listening to me share my heart, he would say to me in his ever-so-kind and always pastorally-supportive tone, "*Dean, if your relationship with your mom does not get fully worked out down here, it'll get worked out in Heaven.*" Whether it was the peace in his voice or the message his voice was sending to me, or maybe a combination of both; either way his encouragement became a Rhema Word that helped me navigate those moments. A Rhema Word is the enlightened Word of God for any given situation and its always an on-time Word from the Lord.

The Rhema Word that Pastor George gave continues to bring comfort to me these days, especially when I go by the cemetery to visit mom's grave. While standing beside it, I think about what it would be like to talk with her now. I wonder how our relationship would be different today, in this very moment, as she is experiencing the purest of love?

While there are still unanswered questions, I do know that there is a spiritual / emotional blockade that I can feel, almost see, that years ago commandeered my heart. I'm realizing that through this process of emptying out, this spiritual and emotional blockage, this generational curse, has been resident in my heart for decades.

If you, too, have experienced emotional abandonment, odds are you probably understand what I'm describing.

This hindrance has had as its evil assignment one primary objective with several secondary plots, all of which were designed to keep me from having and embracing deeply personal connections at the level of the heart. Intimacy. As this blockade grew in strength, I unknowingly allowed it to become a stronghold that prevented my heart from completely trusting God, thereby causing me to buy the lie of self-reliance. For years, I would never let my guard down long enough to then allow the Lord and the fullness of His blessing, and for that matter, people in general, a place of entry into my heart. With all of the above working against me and driven by a real fear of the unknown, I focused on other's shortcomings instead of looking at me and finding out why I felt and acted as I did. As a result, my heart had become like a stone, and I didn't even realize it.

I so hate this generational curse, because for so long, this hindrance and the negative reinforcements that came with it not only successfully blocked me from experiencing true and full intimacy with Jesus, but also with my wife, Lori, with our kids – with everyone. I didn't place this blockade here, but somehow it seems that as my heart continues to soften, I'm seeing life with a healthier perspective. And with this healthier perspective, I feel a responsibility to see the blockade removed by putting faith in the Word of God and by walking and talking with Jesus.

If you know what I'm talking about and/or if you find yourself experiencing what I've just described, it might be a really good idea for you to invite the Holy Spirit, who serves as our Counselor and Guide, to lead you in a digging expedition into the deepest and most hidden areas of your heart. If on this journey into the unknown you happen to discover a heart of stone within yourself that may be the result of a generational curse, the Word of God offers you and I hope. Part of this hope is found in Ezekiel 36:26 which says, *"I will give you a NEW HEART and put a NEW*

SPIRIT within you; I will take the HEART of STONE out of your flesh and give you a HEART of FLESH." I don't know about you but having a new heart that is no longer a heart of stone sure sounds like a good idea to me.

Let's keep going.

I live by the truth of seedtime and harvest; but you know what? I didn't sow the seed to have a generational curse, a spiritual hindrance in my heart. And I sure didn't sow the seed to be emotionally abandoned. As soon as I wrote that last sentence, a cascading flow of more questions immediately follows:

How could I have sown the seed of abandonment? I was four-years-old when I first experienced it.

What was perhaps so wounded or broken inside my mom that would have caused her to turn away from me? Had she been emotionally abandoned? Had she, too, been rejected?

The Word of God teaches us in Genesis 1:11 that *"seeds produce after their kind."* The truth of this verse causes me to compassionately pause and ponder and think about mom and the emotional well-being of her heart. Maybe she, more than anyone else in my life, could fully understand and relate to a lifetime of pain that comes from the same generational curse of the emotional abandonment.

What makes me so sad and at the same time angry is the fact that while I lived 50 years of my life having been ruled and dominated by this condition, it seems my mom may very well have lived within this same state for most of her 80-year life. While we can't do anything at this point that will affect her, we can apply truth from the Word of God and consistently declare what it says about our freedom from the curse as we accept the blessing of the Lord and the completed work of the cross. Here's what I mean:

Hanging on the cross so long ago, Jesus completely destroyed the works of the devil for all of humanity. Suspended between Heaven and earth on that old, wooden cross, with nails being driven into His body, a spear being thrust into His side, and a crown of thorns crushed into his head, the Son of God who became the Son of Man who then became the Son of God once again, died for you and for me. In His death, in that one act of supreme love and unabashed obedience, He took on the curse of sin so that you and I could live in the blessing. More on this later in our time together, but for now let's pick up several years later.

For many, many years growing up as a child and then a teenager, mom would say to me, "You've thrown me under the bus – you're always trying to replace me." By this, mom was saying that because she and I never really emotionally connected with one another, she felt like, in her words, I was trying to replace her with a *mom* with whom I had connection. While I never felt like I was *throwing her under a bus*, I do vividly remember and readily accept as true the fact that I was consistently on a search for a mom, a lady who would love me and be proud of me as an emotionally healthy mom loves and is proud of her son. After all, as a very young teenager I surmised, *you can't replace what you don't have*.

Here's something I've learned. At the core of a stony heart that has experienced emotional abandonment is something oftentimes known as an *orphan spirit*. By definition, an orphan spirit is one that reflects orphans in our world. Think about it, orphans do not become orphans by their own choosing, do they? By definition, something happens to cause a child to become an orphan, a person whose parents are either dead or a person whose parents, for whatever reason, gave them up. Show me a person, either young or old, who is living with an orphan spirit and I'll show you a person who, more times than not, is screaming for acceptance. They are living with an undying and unquenchable need to belong, desperately searching for the approval of someone whom they deem important. With that said, the question that immediately comes to my heart is this: how many people are going through life as emotional orphans today?

31

With that question burning in my thoughts, I now begin to wonder about my own quest to *be enough*. In the early years of life, I, by default, became a performance-based person in an effort to compensate for what I never really felt – the assurance that I was OK just being me; the assurance that I didn't have to DO to BE. This lack of intimate connection, coupled with the stony heart that took up residence early on in my life, were all part of the plan that the devil used to try to keep my heart from the heart of God. The Word says in Romans 8:39 that "… *nothing shall separate us from the love of God which is in Christ Jesus our Lord;* " but somewhere in there, now more than ever, I believe you and I must choose to live in this truth. Otherwise, we can become disconnected from His love. That's convicting.

I'm told by someone whom I trust that I need to "feel"; that the emotions I've been "pushing down" are not a problem that need to find a solution. Feeling is ok. Maybe even healing. But feeling in and of itself will not bring healing to your heart nor to mine. Feeling is an emotion. Healing is a divine act of God; and because of what Jesus has done for us on the cross, that healing is available right here, right now.

In the meantime, in all of this writing, journaling and processing, and with the death of my mom, I've looked at the five stages of emotional grief. They are: denial, bargaining, anger, depression (emotional numbness), and then acceptance. As I look at these five stages, I'm sad that mom is no longer with us, but I'm not angry that she died. Unless Jesus returns before our appointed time, all of us will one day take our last breath and die. Death is part of life. Where mom's death is concerned, I've been angry at the *finality* of death here on earth. Angry that so much died with my mom. So much was buried when her casket was lowered into the earth and *fresh dirt* thrown on top of *old pain*.

And then there's that word depression. Oh, how that word irritates me – to me, it's never a confession that should be made (*I'm depressed* – just invites depression to set up residence in the heart of the one confessing – again, the *confession brings possession* thing – the words we speak create the world in which we then live.).

As it was explained to me, depression as it relates to the grieving process, is more about feeling **numb**. Sounds better, doesn't it? And feeling numb, as I shared earlier - now that's an emotion that I know something about. I've been told over and over by my wife that for years, I would just "numb out". When a person numbs out, it can send the message that they really just don't care. But for me, it's not that I haven't cared; it's the necessity of having a break from **caring too much**, which is a form of pride. Well, to be blunt, it's sin. At the heart of pride is the belief, or at least the actions that say, "*I've got this.*" When a person hits the runway of pride, truth is they don't "*got this*". *It has them*.

That being said, since the Word of God, the Bible, teaches us that we are **not** supposed to carry or take on the cares of life, then what exactly are we supposed to do when we encounter situations that in our natural world like coming face-to-face with an emotional and spiritual hindrance that's been stealthily operating in your life for five decades, causes *care* to be the natural choice to pursue? Thankfully we have that answer as 1 Peter 5:7 plainly instructs us to, "*Cast all your care upon Him, for He cares for you.*" "Him" and "He" are both capitalized, and because they are, the Bible is referring to Jesus. What are we supposed to do with situations that want us to give into the temptation of taking on the care? Here's the answer. By faith, *cast* that care onto **Jesus** and say, *You've got this, Lord*. Once we cast it onto Him, leave it with Him and really trust that He's got it.

Going through this journaling process, which, remember, is causing me to slow down and actually *feel*, along with the time I'm investing with the Lord and in the Word of God, the stony heart that has been resident within me for so very long is being replaced with a new heart of flesh. And if He'll do it for me, He'll do it for you … as long as you and I do things His way.

For me, for the majority of my life up until recently, the pain of "feeling" sometimes was just too much to bear and the momentary anesthesia of *numbing out* has provided a few minutes or hours of relief. Numbing out comes in many, many forms. Some people numb out with alcohol. Others numb out with drugs. Many find food and overeating an escape that provides what later is revealed for what it truly is – a *false sense* of escape. For me, my *numbing out* never came in the form of substance abuse or an addiction. It was something just as damaging, though. I numbed out by shutting down and living life with a pride that had as its calling card a falsely elevated sense of superiority.

The thing about pride is it is both subtle and at the same time, it can be an in your face, over the top, announcement to anyone who has ears to hear and eyes to see that the **BIG I** is in the room. Pride screams for attention. It has to be noticed. It must be validated. And if this required validation is not offered, then the person in whom the tentacles of pride are fiercely clutching will always find a way to ensure the perceived validation is given by anyone or everyone in the room.

To the emotionally unhealthy, spiritually depleted, and physically exhausted teenager or adult, this perceived validation of pride comes in many forms: what I do; what I have; whom I know; who knows me; what I wear; what I drive; etc. So ugly. Pride requires, it must have, an unhealthy dose of attention from others. It feeds on it.

Please do not miss what you are about to read. The void that my heart experienced having suffered for so many decades with this spiritual and emotional hindrance has simultaneously been fortified and guarded by pride. Pride refuses to let love in, and it rarely lets love out. Pride deceptively says that because we really believe that "I've got this", we therefore do not need love. Nothing can be further from the truth. We all need to experience and give love. It's a faith force that demands fostering, and according to 1 Corinthians 13:8, "*Love never fails.*"

Oh, what a web of deceit the enemy spun in my life and maybe in your life, too. There is only one way out of the assignments of the enemy, and it's found in John 8:32 where we are told: "*And you shall know the truth, and the truth shall make us free.*" Don't miss what you just read. The **truth** we know is the **truth** that sets us free. We must have, embrace, receive and speak more truth from the Word of God.

As I journal and do so from this place of deep, deep honesty, something is shifting. I know that merely writing in and of itself does not cause this shift. It's the presence of the One who defeated the source of pride Who is leading me to write; the same One who placed His hands on my shoulders when I began this journey; the One who is giving me the words to declare, words that have begun the passage of unlocking that which has been buried for so very long. Let's keep going.

What's the opposite of pride? Humility. A long time ago a counselor I was talking with offered me this definition of humility: "*no pretense*". Here's how Websters defines pretense – "A false reason or explanation that is used to hide the real purpose of something. An act or appearance that looks real but is false." And so, as I'm living life with **no pretense**, then I'm doing so authentically and with no agenda of trying to create a false or elevated narrative or perception of who I am and what I am doing. As a Christian who is choosing to live life without pretense, it offers me the opportunity to consistently be the real me; and as I do, become ok with who I am because, *it is no longer I who lives but He who lives in me.*

And you know what? As a born-again Believer in Jesus, living your life with no pretense and being who God called you to be can likewise lead you directly into meeting and getting to know the real you. Believe me; you getting to know the real you is a journey you do not want to miss.

The entrance of Your Word brings light comes to my heart at this moment, because it's words that deliver insight and revelation into a heart that has been so locked up for all of these years. And with the unlocking of my heart, a new question migrates to the forefront of my mind:

What does life look like when there is no bondage, when there is nothing left to prove; when true joy far supersedes momentary happiness, when the emotional and spiritual blockage has been removed from me as far as the east is from the west; when the curse bows to the blessing?

Living life with no bondage, with nothing left to prove, with no care. Living life with true joy. That, my friend, is the life Jesus desires for you and me. In spiritual terms, maybe we would call this kind of living the GRACE LIFE. A life not based on our function and productivity, but rather a life that is totally founded upon what Jesus has already done for and made available to you and me – that my friend is the BLESSING God offers.

The closer we move into living life for Him instead of for ourselves, isn't it refreshing to see that He's right here, right now, totally accessible to anyone who moves toward Him? Want in on a secret? He's been here all along. I've realized that I have complete access to Jesus and to His peace; not because I've accomplished everything on my TO DO list but rather, because He lives in my heart. With Jesus as the King of my heart, I'm at real peace *with me*; and as I am, I can sit with myself in the quietness of life and as I do, I don't freak out, jump up, and go do something that makes me feel better about myself. How does this happen? It's all because He is peace, and the more I'm hanging out with Him, the less time I waste trying to be someone and something He never intended me to be.

It's as though I am on the authentic journey that leads me to the freedom *to be me.* It's a journey that I encourage you, too, to consider embracing.

And so, there is the promise of a new day. And with this new day, once again, questions come fast.

But how do I get there?

What is required of me to live life with nothing to prove and with no need for public or for that matter private validation from people? Just Jesus.

What's the roadmap?

Where do I begin?

Maybe in writing, maybe just maybe, I'm further along in this journey than I realized. That thought brings a smile to my face and provides the courage to keep on emptying onto this screen what has been so deeply buried in my once stony heart.

And as I empty out, whether it's the emotional abandonment, having been sexually abused as a teenager, living life with anger, the fear of letting go and wholly trusting God, or the eradication of a generational curse from my family and me, I want you to know that everything you are about to read and hopefully discover is written with one goal – for you to find the spiritual and emotional freedom that only comes from truly knowing and yielding to Him.

And so, as we continue, I offer you the gift of courage – the courage to turn the page, to keep reading, and to see if what you read can be part of the roadmap that Jesus takes you on as you travel your very own journey. For me, my journey took a turn when I was singing at six years old.

SINGING AT SIX YEARS OLD

Some of my earliest memories of childhood began for me when I was four years old. It still amazes me that after all of these years, one particular day is as fresh on my heart right now as it was the day I lived it; no doubt, more so. It was about 9 am on the morning of Saturday, December 13th, 1969, the day after my sister, Deanna, was born. It was on this Saturday that dad took me on a very, very special outing. As he and I walked across the asphalt parking lot and into the hospital that windy and cold December morning, the day I got to officially meet my sister, my left hand was tightly clutching his right hand and my right hand was fiercely holding onto a strand of ribbons that were wholly reserved for the head of jet black hair that Deanna was born with. These ribbons would become the very first gift ever given to my sister.

As I walked into that hospital room, I caught my first glimpse of mom holding her and I remember a feeling coming over me that was unmistakable to ignore and at four years old, equally impossible for me to define. I now know that right there, in that moment, with absolutely no idea what to do with what I was experiencing in my heart, the excitement and joy that was in my heart only moments earlier as we rode in the elevator up to mom's hospital room gave way to a stark realization that would later be identified as emotional detachment from me, initiated by my mom. And it would stretch for decades. Mom was now holding the child in her arms that years later, she would publicly say about, ***"One good investment is worth a lifetime of work."***

This emotional detachment was the first of a number of traumatic events that would ultimately define multiple seasons of my life; and as they did, the pain, the results of the pain, and the internal message of emotional abandonment would again and again become so clear in my mind; the message that was the generational curse assigned to my life by the enemy ... ***I wasn't enough.***

Let's be very, very clear. Even though trauma has occurred in me and to me, I do not want you to think that this unleashing of the plan of the enemy in my life excuses me and exempts me from my behavior. To say that "the devil made me do it" is both childish and wrong. Jesus paid too heavy of a price for us to then cheapen His sacrifice by our announcing to anyone and everyone that our actions are the result of the devil. We all have the freedom to choose how we live life, and the choices we make then create the circumstances in which we live. Here's the point I want to share with you – emotional trauma is real and left undealt with and/or ignored, it does not go away on its own nor do we become magically healed from it. This notwithstanding, for the person who refuses to look at himself or herself and the choices they make and instead chooses to ascribe their lives to the devil and his attacks and to what other people do or don't do, this person will live in a lie until they come face-to-face with the truth and then with themselves. And then, they have to choose how they are going to live moving forward. I know this to be all too true, because it has happened to me.

For now, let's go forward about two years to when I was six years old, living with mom and dad and my two-year-old sister at 6404 Julie Lane in Chattanooga, Tennessee. Ours was a quaint street that was home to eight growing families. I remember that one of our neighbors was in full time ministry and he was gone from home a lot. Another neighbor was retired. Across the street lived an engineer and his wife and their two children. And down the street lived Chris Frank and his family. Chris and I were best friends growing up and he, more than anyone, awakened within me a love for sports. He and I played together almost every day, from sun up to sun down.

All of the houses in our small, little neighborhood were about the same size; it was the kind of neighborhood where kids were free to run and roam and play all day long. We were limited only by our imaginations; and on any given day, our imaginations carried us into the wild, wild West; onto the gridiron of professional football fields; and into the far-flung galaxies of space that were yet to be discovered.

Life with my friends was so much fun those days; but in the evenings as the summer sun began to set in the western sky and my time to return home in time for family dinners quickly approached, I oftentimes found myself wanting to linger a little longer, lingering in the world I was creating in my mind versus returning home. In the years to come, my creating alternative world realities would become a way of life for me; a "fantasy world" as mom would later refer to them; but again, more on that later.

At six years old, reality for me was living life constantly being propelled into a lifestyle of personal perfectionism, striving to meet a need on my own that I was incapable of meeting. In the years to come, this self-absorption would become an out-of-control way of life as, by default, my personality recognized that when I wasn't getting something I needed from mom or someone else I deemed important, I would set out to meet my needs, on my own, irrespective of my then limited life experiences. Attempting to meet our own needs is a vital component to identify within this generational curse. It was in these early years of my attempting to meet my own needs that the seed of pride we talked about in the last chapter was taking root in the soil of my heart.

You see, because I lived with such a deep sense of insecurity, I felt like I never quite fit in. Because I didn't, I was constantly striving for something, something a six-year-old was unable to identify, much less try to understand. Irrespective of my inability to understand what was going on with the derailment and sabotage of my emotional development, that demonic assignment of my need for mom's approval, was becoming more and more obvious, and this need was only increasing, not decreasing.

This need was magnified and my attempt to meet this need on my own embarrassingly played out on one particular summer morning when I ventured into the creation of a moment that I just *knew* would work. Here's what happened.

The sun was shining early that Monday morning as I eagerly awaited the arrival of a very special guest into our home. A lady on whom I remember so desperately wanting to make a good impression. What made this guest special? Just twenty-four hours earlier, I had sat in our church and listened as she sang a solo in front of a packed out auditorium, and now this very pretty lady with the voice that seemed to touch such a deep place in my heart was only minutes away from knocking on our front door. Prior to our guest arriving, however, mom informed me that our home *needed* to be cleaned. Let's be clear. It was clean, but the necessity for perfectionism drove my mom, and by default, me, to always go the extra mile to ensure the best impression was consistently put forth.

Now only minutes away from our guest's arrival, I was vacuuming our family room and simultaneously very aware that at any minute a knock on our door would be heard. That knock was my cue to begin singing, singing at the top of my voice so that our guest was sure to hear. After all, I reasoned if I wanted this lady with a voice of an angel to *recognize* and *accept* me, then we surely must share something in common. In my six-year-old mind, we undoubtedly shared a love for music and voices that drew people into our presence. Of course, it never crossed my mind that singing in public may not have been a gift the Lord had given me.

And then it happened. The knock came, mom opened the door, and our guest walked in. My heart was racing but this was the moment for which I had been preparing all morning. This was it, and on cue I took a deep breath and began to sing. I sang a song I had learned in church and I put my whole heart into my *performance*. To my astonishment and then embarrassment, with every word I sang, it was as if our guest did not hear one word coming out of my mouth. For that matter, she never even acknowledged that I was singing. It was as if my voice did not exist to her. Her response was the exact opposite of what I had so desired to see happen and ultimately experience. My desire? To have this lady acknowledge, accept, and embrace me as a six-year-old little boy who so desperately wanted to feel loved. That surely didn't happen, and I was crushed, again. My heart sank and my face turned red. I could feel as the heat of embarrassment was rushing across my face and all I could think to do was escape from our home and flee to the *fantasy world* that awaited me outside. The generational curse was at work.

I excused myself and *just* made it outside before bursting into tears. From that day forward, my escaping public moments to live out and experience private pain became a norm for me that would not change for many, many years. Standing outside alone on that Monday morning with tears cascading down my cheeks, I wondered why our guest had shown no interest in me or my attempt to impress her. Again, the question that awaited an answer was front and center in my heart and on my mind: ***Why wasn't I enough?***

If you have ever wrestled with the question of wondering why you weren't enough, then you can probably understand that for many years following that Monday morning meltdown I did my best to limit the opportunities to ever again purposefully allow my heart to be so terribly exposed to such embarrassment and pain. In fact, I so deeply buried the pain and recklessly chose to ignore the embarrassment, choosing instead to create the *fantasy world* of the life I *wanted* to live, that I became addicted to an emotional drug that you might recognize yourself. My emotional drug of choice? Lying.

Today, as I look back over those next seven to nine years of my constant lying, I do so with great empathy for those teenagers and their families who have fallen into the trap of not feeling like they're enough. In their effort to overcompensate for what they were never given, so many of these teens are swimming in the deepest portions of a turbulent, emotional ocean and are wearing themselves out past the point of exhaustion. How? By trying to meet their own emotional and physical needs with lying so much that they eventually are void of the truth and actually begin to believe their own lies.

I know this to be true, because it is exactly what happened to me. As a teenager I lied more than I ever told the truth. In fact, I lied so much during the teenage season of my life that *you had to catch me telling the truth.* I lied when it made no sense to lie. I lied about our family's income, about the type of home we lived in, about the girls I dated; but most of all, I lied to my parents, especially my mom, about my grades; grades that I earned during my prep school experience.

MY PREP SCHOOL EXPERIENCE

Before diving deep into my prep school experience, it's important to recognize that just as is the case in all of my relationships, my experience at this prep school was neither all good nor was it all bad. It's a premiere school that offers those who attend the opportunity to excel above and beyond their wildest and most imaginative dreams.

For the young people who maybe aren't quite wired for a prep school experience but are sent there anyway, well, for them, going there can be a journey into a world that they, too, recognize is beyond their wildest and most imaginative dreams. In these instances, however, it's not dreams, its nightmares. I would be counted among the latter, not the former. Here's some of what happened.

Growing up, where I would go to middle and high school was never in doubt, at least not as far as my parents were concerned. In fact, when I was only two weeks old, my application for enrollment was already on file in this prep school's Office of Admissions.

Mom would oftentimes share with Deanna and me that as a teenager herself, she had always so admired the students who were the product of a prep school education. Many of these students could become titans of business, elected officials, engineers, doctors, attorneys, college professors, ministers of the Gospel. In fact, a large percentage of those who have attended this particular prep school have done so as part of a family rite of passage. Generations of family members before them have walked the hallowed halls and lived in the dorms and competed on the numerous athletic fields that comprise the sprawling academic community.

All of the above notwithstanding, what I remember with intense clarity is the Saturday morning my parents dropped me off at this school where I would join hundreds of others as we assembled to receive instructions prior to taking the hours-long Entrance Exam. The internal pressure I felt and the emotional baggage that was resident in my heart that day were both off the charts. There was no joy for me in this experience. In fact, there was dread. (Soon, dread would become the most recognizable emotion with which I lived life.) What was in me was a foreboding fear of questions that began with arguably the two most feared words on the planet - "*What If?*"

What if I didn't do well on the test?

What if I didn't complete the test in the allotted time?

What if my letters of recommendation were not strong enough?

But without any hesitation of contradiction, the looming *what if* question that I could not shake from my thoughts that Saturday morning was that same old question I'd now rehearsed over and over for years – What if I wasn't *good enough* to get in, to be accepted?

In other words, what if *I wasn't enough*?

You see, in my life, not being accepted, not being enough, was the natural progression of emotional abandonment and it's the fruit that grows from the root of this generational curse. Sadly, many, many decades of life would come and go before I summoned the courage to allow and ultimately accept into my heart the whole BLESSING of the Lord. One of the benefits that come with this BLESSING is intimacy with my heavenly Father, an intimacy that completely replaces the *orphan spirit* that lives within the generational curse of emotional abandonment and sexual abuse. If you find that you are living with this orphan spirit, don't give up. There is hope, and His name is Jesus, who, according to Colossians 1:27, is the hope of glory. ("*To them God willed to make known what are the riches of the glory of this mystery among the Gentiles: which is Christ in you, the hope of glory.*")

Let's now go forward to another Saturday morning about six weeks after I had taken the entrance exam when a letter arrived in our mailbox. I remember standing in our driveway, intently watching the expressions on my mom's face as she tore into that prep school envelope and read the first three words of the letter, "Dear Dean, Congratulations …" Mom shouted with joy, and in that moment, I somehow knew that my life had just changed. A forced smile came across my face as I saw how happy mom was but, in spite of her happiness I was experiencing a sinking feeling in the deepest places of my heart that what I had just been accepted into was not going to be a journey that would end well.

In all fairness to my mom and dad, never once did I voice my concerns and never once did I stand up and say that I liked the school I was in presently and I really did not want to go to this prep school. Open communication was a point of weakness for me in our family, and yet again this lack of communication was all part of the generational curse that had been assigned to my life. And to this point, whether you're single, a parent, or a teenager reading this book, I strongly encourage you to incorporate this truth from the Word of God into your life, right here, right now: OPEN COMMUNICATION PERMITS PROGRESS. Don't assume anything. Instead pray about everything; and as you do, take time to openly, honestly, and in love communicate with the people in your life, especially your family. And when it comes to communication, I'm reminded that two-thirds of communicating is found in the art of listening. By design, God created us with two eyes, two ears, but only one mouth. And to this end, maybe we all would become more effective in communication if we listened twice as much as we talked.

Now, back to my prep school experience.

Whether I wanted to go or not didn't matter. I was now enrolled as a student, and through a number of conversations that she and I had, mom made sure I understood that my responsibility was to study and excel in this opportunity to go to a school that

46

few others were fortunate enough to attend, i.e. pay the price. And so, thus began a new season of extreme pressure and my trying to measure up, to be enough, and to be accepted ... on my own.

From day one, I loved *saying* that I went to my new school – saying so seemed to feed that empty hole in my heart that came from emotional abandonment, a hole that, at that point in my young life, was only expanding and growing. Even though I so enjoyed the response that people, young and old alike, gave me when I matter-of-factly shared where I went to school, I was in no way interested in the two - three hours of homework that I brought home every single night. As mom would later tell me on a regular basis as my grades plummeted due to a lack of effort on my part, I wasn't willing to *pay the price*, not just as a student, but later on in life those same exact words, *you're not willing to pay the price*, became the resounding message that was communicated to me. Again, what I was doing and who I was becoming *wasn't enough*. The curse was at work.

For me, the workload and the pressure to perform at school only added to the ever-increasing insecurity with which I lived. And because my grades reflected my lack of dedicated, nightly studying, it didn't take long for me to become the target of daily bullying from my peers, especially from those students who were *paying the price* to excel in their schoolwork. Imagine being at a prep school where excelling in academics was not only accepted as the norm, but also expected. This bullying only added fuel to the raging internal fire known as peer pressure, a pressure that I would learn to try and *manage* almost every single day for years to come.

But here's the thing about you and I managing internal pressure, and I'm sure you probably already know this; we are not capable on our own of managing the growing, internal pressures that life throws our way. Truth-be-told, for the person not yet sold out to Jesus and His grace on their life, that pressure is managing them and is doing so relentlessly. As it does, if we do not yield to the GRACE LIFE referenced earlier, a life not based on our function and productivity but rather, a life that is totally founded upon what Jesus has already done for and made available to you and me, we then try to shoulder all of these emotions and their corresponding results on our own. As a result, we find that in and of ourselves, we are completely incapable of doing so. All of us, irrespective of our calling, our purpose, were created to be dependent upon the One who is greater than the sum total of all He created.

And yet in our attempts to be totally self-sufficient, whether knowingly or unknowingly, we literally are by default turning our backs on Jesus, and that, my friend, is the supreme goal of any generational curse. But fear not, because even if we have turned our back on Him, He will never turn His back on us. Why won't He turn His back on us? Because it's a promise He's given us that we see in Hebrews 13:5: "... *For He Himself has said, 'I will never leave you nor forsake you.*" In His perfect timing, when He knows we're ready to see a glimpse of the *big picture*, He very lovingly pulls back the spiritual blinders from across our spiritual eyes and allows us to discover the truth that we don't *got this* and desperately need our heavenly Father. In that moment, our Spirit then cries out for Abba Father to be not only our Father, but also, our Dad. Maybe you find yourself wondering about the difference between a father and a dad. If so, here's something for you to consider. Dads give us what we **want** while fathers give us what we **need**. Let's continue.

With the peer pressure only increasing in the classroom, the one area at school where I did excel and enjoyed a moderate level of success was being part of the school's tennis team. And so, I devoted what little emotional energy and physical strength I did have into playing tennis every afternoon from 3 pm until 5 pm. My diligence on the courts paid off, as I became a contributing member of the team, eventually earning a Letter Jacket in tennis. Through this sport, I proved to myself that when I was willing to *pay the price*, I could be competitive with my peers. That truth would mean much to me in the years to come, and it's a truth that generational curses never want exposed.

What I'm getting ready to say is something I share every day on the road when speaking with teenagers and young adults. Ready? *If you and I do not deal with our emotions, our emotions will deal with us.* Two and a half years into this routine of school, being bullied, playing tennis, periodical late-night studying, and absolutely not dealing with my emotions, my world came crashing down. One afternoon as I was physically exhausted from the emotional pain with which I lived, I collapsed on a tennis court and could not get up while playing a match against another school. After everyone watching realized that I had not tripped nor had I fallen, but yet I wasn't getting up, a few minutes of awkward silence set in.

My opponent stood across the net, wondering what to do. My coach came running out to check on me; but because it was emotional exhaustion and not a physical injury, I did not yet have the knowledge or the emotional tools to adequately communicate with him what I was feeling or not feeling as I was lying there on the ground. But what I could do was read the non-verbal communication being sent my way from the stands. You see, mom was in the audience watching my match that day; and as I was laying there on my stomach in the afternoon heat, I looked into the stands and our eyes connected. When they did, she gave me a look, a non-verbal instruction, to rise from that concrete surface and continue playing my match. And so, that's exactly what I did. I lost that tennis match that day, but somewhere deep within my heart, I also lost hope in any meaningful relationship with mom. From that day forward and for many years to come, ours would be a surface relationship, one that would cause even more pain to both mom and me. The generational curse of emotional abandonment, the orphan spirit that had a firm grip on my life, was now operating in a way and with a power that would only be stopped decades later if and when I came face-to-face with a personal choice to surrender to what Jesus had already done for me.

Not long after my meltdown on the tennis court, my parents, at the suggestion of our family doctor, checked me into a local hospital where I would spend the next four and a half days undergoing a battery of testing, all of which were searching for what was making me so tired. Even though I was in the hospital being treated for exhaustion, in an effort to ensure I didn't miss out on my studies, mom made sure each day to go by the school, meet my teachers, and then bring my books and daily assignments to the hospital. To offer you an idea of our pace of learning at this prep school, I missed six chapters in my Science class while in the hospital ... and that was just one of my five classes.

As a side note, back in 1978, society showed little public interest in treating teenagers for emotional sickness and so, while having all of these medical tests run on my physical body, no medical professional was paying any attention whatsoever to my emotional health. In contrast to 1978, today's teens are diagnosed and treated with prescription drugs at alarmingly high rates for both mental illness as well as emotional trauma. Somewhere in all of this there lives a tension, a balance between ignorance, denial, and overtreatment.

At the conclusion of my stay at Parkridge Hospital, a hospital that six and a half years later, in what would become one of the most ironic moments in my life, as I rushed my mom back there in an attempt to save her life, my doctor discharged me with the diagnosis of hypoglycemia (low blood sugar).

Three weeks later, because I had fallen so far behind in all of my classes and despite the immediate implementation of a consistent nutritional regimen created for hypoglycemic patients, my parents realized that if something did not change both dramatically and immediately, I was going to fail the ninth grade. And so, in an effort to avoid my failing and having to repeat a grade, along with the personal embarrassment that my family would surely encounter, a decision was made to pull me out of this prep school and enroll me in a local Christian school. My life went from bad to worse, literally overnight.

I remember my first day at this new school; nervously walking into this new environment; completely unaware that news had already spread to some of these students that my leaving my previous school is what saved me from having to repeat my freshman year of high school. It didn't take long for the jokes and the bullying to begin. And so, almost from day one at this new school, I was trying my best to create a narrative that these teachers and students would buy, all in an effort to salvage my severely damaged reputation. To do so, I created a false image to fend off the verbal jabs that were once again becoming daily doses of pain and embarrassment and to convince myself that despite my obvious failure, somehow, some way, maybe *I was enough.*

This is the time and place where my lying to people became an addiction that exploded with creativity and tales that were larger than life. It was here that I resorted to what I knew best – living life in the *fantasy world* that mom oftentimes referred to, a world where I lied about anything and everything. After all, I surmised, lying to these kids couldn't hurt them or me, because I was only going to be in this small, Christian school for a few months.

After a quick summer and our annual family vacation to Daytona Beach, Florida, August came quickly and with the opening day of school, I was right back at the prep school. To my astonishment, my life immediately picked up exactly where I had left it months earlier when my parents had pulled me out and sent me to the Christian school. Any hope that the bullying and verbal harassment would have disappeared or at the very least, mercifully been redirected to someone else, anyone else, was quickly annihilated when, after our opening chapel on the first day of school, I was pummeled with unimaginable amounts of attention from any number of students who simply could not believe that I had come back for another year. For that matter, it was hard for me to believe I had willfully and dutifully returned; but once again, the belief was that in doing so, all of this was eventually going to work out for my good. Eventually ….

What no one planned, however, was that in two short months, I would be leaving this prep school for the last time as a student. By October of that year, my grades were horrific, my strength was again zapped, and my emotions were frayed. Remember, if you and I do not deal with our emotions, our emotions will deal with us; and at this point, I surely had not dealt with mine.

Mom now understood that something was really wrong, and she and dad immediately went into crisis management mode; getting a plan and systematically working that plan. They took me out and enrolled me back at Boyd-Buchanan High School, the school where I had been a student from grades two through six. Being back at Boyd-Buchanan brought its own set of challenges with some mean students who initially wanted to hurt my feelings by bullying me. In comparison to what I had just endured, though, it was evident to my parents and to me that this was where I needed to be … I was genuinely happy.

Within weeks of returning to Boyd-Buchanan, I was chosen to be the editor-in-chief of our school newspaper, I was President of the Pep Club, I was in the Chorus and Show Chorus, and I was Stage Managing our school play, HELLO DOLLY! And somewhere in between all of the above, I managed to earn really good grades and make some genuine friends.

For the first time in a long, long time, I was smiling and enjoying school. In my mind this was how life was supposed to be. Finally, I was popular, I was going on dates, I was playing tennis again, and because of my increasing friend group in our youth department, church was something I looked forward to each week.

As a side note, even though she was terribly disappointed that I had not graduated from the prep school, mom's disappointment was partially eradicated years later when our local newspaper did a feature article on our ministry. In it the writer reported about my being a national, inspirational speaker who focused our mission, message and ministry on ministering hope to teenagers in high schools through assemblies and chapels. As a result of that article, I was invited to return to the prep school I had attended years ago and speak to the entire student body and faculty. Standing at the rostrum I allowed my eyes to span that vast auditorium full of students with bright eyes and keen minds who that day were seated where many years earlier I once sat. I wondered what had changed there since I had been a student. I thought about the young people seated throughout that chapel and wondered who the ones were excelling in academics; who were the ones making it happen on the athletic fields. I wondered who the bullies were, and I thought about those who were being bullied. I was so very thankful to have this opportunity to be back and share our message of hope with them.

As it was now time to share my remarks, I quickly prayed that somehow, some way, what I was about to say would resonate with the entire audience.

With those thoughts migrating across my mind and just before sharing my opening sentence, I glanced down to the front row where mom was seated, and her smile of approval offered me the fuel to speak with both passion and confidence. When my time with the students came to a close that day, they not only had listened, they also had heard, and as such very graciously gave a standing ovation in response to what I had just spoken about. Walking out of the chapel with mom, she quietly said to me, "What you just gave me was worth all of the tuition your dad and I paid for you to be at this school. Thank you, Dean." I was genuinely happy for mom that day.

As the second semester of my sophomore year at Boyd–Buchanan began, life at home for me was much less pressured, and I was as content as I could have been having not yet dealt with my emotions. Little did I know it then, but the generational curse was about to rise its ugly head again; and when it did, this time it would do so in a way that I would forever remember. It was sixty seconds that changed my life.

PART THREE

THE ABUSE

SIXTY SECONDS THAT CHANGED MY LIFE

The school bell rang, and I could hardly wait to make a quick exodus from my last class period of the day. Wednesdays were always such long days: up by 6:45 am; breakfast by 7:15 am; at school by 7:45 am; classes began at 8 am with our weekly chapel service commencing right after first period. All day at school and then dinner at church, a youth service, and then home to do homework before finally calling it a day.

A little of the back-story. Even though I was really excelling in school and my friend base was growing, the devil made sure that the lunch period was rarely an enjoyable one for me. Irrespective of what was going on throughout my school day, it was as if the LED targets to be bullied lit up across my back when it was time for lunch. (This, too, was part of that demonic assignment we've been talking about throughout our time together.)

During those terrifying thirty minutes that so many students continue to live through today, all I wanted to do was get into the lunchroom, find some level of obscurity, eat my lunch, and get to the next class of the day. As ours was a smaller school and the lunchroom was readily accessible by our students, my attempt at and desire for personal obscurity in the lunchroom many days proved to be next to impossible.

You may be a teenager who can totally relate or your teenage years have long since come and gone without major drama; but, nonetheless you find yourself reliving your very own *lunchroom* experience right here, right now. No matter where you are and despite your age, if you are the survivor of peer-based bullying, you know what I'm describing to be absolutely the truth.

Today as a Speaker who specializes in ministering to teenagers, I often have the opportunity of sitting with students after finishing up one of our assembly programs or chapel services in their respective high schools. In doing so, we get the honor of offering a safe space for members of this generation to open up and freely share some of those deep, dark places in their own heart. For some, it's bullying; for others, it's challenges at home with mom and dad. For a growing number of students, it's the contemplation of suicide; and for many, it's sexual abuse. As I listen with sincere empathy to every student with whom I sit, many, many times after leaving those conversations, I find myself going back in time to one of the darkest and most confusing experiences I have ever experienced. As I do, I'm ever mindful of and grateful for a promise we have in Genesis 50:20 which says, *"But as for you, you meant evil against me; but God meant it for good, in order to bring it about as it is this day, to save MANY PEOPLE alive."* The *evil* that was brought against me was an experience that took place on a Wednesday afternoon after school, and it would ultimately become sixty seconds that changed the entire trajectory of my life. This is when the generational curse intensified.

On this particular day, our Wednesday afternoon classes dragged on and on and on until finally, at 3:10 pm, the bell rang, signifying that another day of my high school experience was behind me. Choosing to instead focus on the fun that was scheduled for that afternoon rather than the lunchroom bullying and the homework that awaited me later that night, I hopped into the car of a friend of mine from church. This person was 17, an only child, and drove a fast sports car. Our plan for the afternoon was to run over to my friend's house, play some sports, and be back at church in time for family dinner at 6 pm.

We quickly got to my friend's very large three-story home, said hello to family, and I was invited to a bedroom to see a new electronic gadget my friend had been given the previous weekend. When the door was shut, I remember thinking that was a little weird, but that new gadget had my full attention. My friend invited me to sit down on the bed; and as I did, my naïveté must have been on full display. I never saw coming what happened next. Like a masterful magician whose sly hands moved like the wind, my abuser's hands were all over me. I was stunned. I had no idea what was happening or what I should or even could do to stop this assault. It was as if I suddenly had no voice. Literally, I was silenced. Sixty seconds later, it was over. My abuser got up, looked at me, smiled and said, "Want to go downstairs now and play ping pong?" I still could not speak, so I nodded in approval, and we played a few games where I played in a state of complete bewilderment. We got back in my friend's sports car, drove to church, walked in, and ate family dinner together … as if nothing had even happened.

Those sixty seconds were a significant part of that demonic assignment on my life; but this time, though, it wasn't just emotional abandonment that was used as the attack of the enemy. No, this time it was the wounds of a faithful friend. And the wounds were deep. Immediately following the abuse, I felt guilty and at the same time, betrayed and confused. And here's where the confusion from the enemy flooded my heart: I really did not know what to do. What I did know, though, was what I **was not** going to do. I was not going to tell anyone what had happened to me. As a fifteen-year-old teenager, I made the subconscious decision to *deny* to myself that anything had happened. I figured that *if I didn't talk about it, then surely it didn't happen.* This season of denial was such a big part of the generational curse expanding into other areas of my life.

Why denial? Why not talk about it with someone? For me to share with anyone what had happened would require a level of trust that brought with it complete confidence that my heart was safe with whomever I was sharing my story. As I took the time to examine all of the people in my life, I once again sadly found myself all alone, totally isolated, and with no one in whom I felt safe enough to confide. If you have experienced trauma on any level, especially sexual abuse, I imagine that you fully understand and embrace as true the necessity of having that person in your life in whom you have total confidence.

And then, just like all the times before when traumatic events had come for a visit in my life, here came the questions.

Why did this happen to me?

Why do bad things happen to good people?

Should I tell anyone what happened?

Am I going to get into trouble for this?

Did I cause this?

Almost immediately following the abuse and all the unanswered questions, not only did I feel like I wasn't enough, now I felt dirty, ashamed, and most of all, I felt DAMAGED. And just like me, if you have experienced sexual abuse, you have your own story that you have lived or are living today, and no one can relive or tell your story in full detail the way you can. It really is uniquely yours. What you can consider doing now is what I put off doing for some twenty-two long, painful and oftentimes disappointing years. You can pray. You can declare healing scriptures over your life. And you can make the choice to open up and genuinely and transparently talk with someone whom you trust and allow them into the individual story that is YOU. I highly recommend professional Christian Counselors who specialize is trauma recovery. Remember what we shared earlier, *open communication permits progress.*

From that fateful Wednesday afternoon forward, I made a vow that I would never again be hurt like that. To ensure the pain of more rejection would not come, I assumed that if people did not know the *real* me and if I deliberately never let anyone close, I'd be safe. So, I habitually reverted back to the lifestyle I had always lived. I once again increased my ever-evolving *fantasy world* stories. I embellished what I did and lied about life experiences.

Then something happened that I never saw coming and at that point in my life had no understanding as to why it was happening. Older girls, high school seniors in general and young ladies in college in specific, began reaching out to me; and as they did, I began dating them, many of them. I was drawn to them in unhealthy ways. They, too, saw something in me, and what they saw, they were drawn to. As a fifteen and then sixteen year-old-teenager, I could not figure out why so many of them were suddenly interested in me. Years later, as I took time to go deep into a prolonged discovery mode of searching for what made me tick and understanding why I had done what I had done, the Holy Spirit, who is our Counselor, showed me that when my sexual abuse occurred, an evil spirit from the enemy was released into my life. This spirit in turn attracted similar evil spirits that yearned to connect and be together. Much in the same way that healthy attracts healthy, I learned that unhealthy attracts unhealthy. This, too, was part of the generational curse that was active in my life. Maybe this revelation is helping you make better sense and/or maybe confirming what you already suspected of why certain people might be in your life.

During this prolonged season for me, I didn't care who I hurt as long as I got the recognition my ever-so-damaged heart was screaming for. Later in life I would learn from lots of time in prayer, in the Word, and in counseling that *pain seeks pleasure*. Because I was in such deep emotional pain and experiencing the voice in my mind that loudly declared that once again, *I wasn't enough*, my need for pleasure was at an all-time high.

As I was dating these older girls, I continued lying all the time. Somewhere along this journey of living in a *fantasy world*, I really lost my way. First and foremost, I lost my heart for God. I lost my desire to let anyone into my own heart, and then I lost me. In place of me, my replacement was a plastic, non-feeling, arrogant young man who cared for no one and nothing. If ever you have lived life like this or if today you find yourself slipping into this lifestyle, I hope you will *remember* something that I had *forgotten* – God and His love will NEVER leave or forsake you, no matter what. The BLESSING of the Lord will always be more powerful than the curse of the enemy.

Let's stay right here on the subject of love for a quick moment. The Bible teaches us in Mark 12:30 to first and foremost, **love** the Lord your God with all your heart, with all your soul, and with all your mind. And then it teaches us to, **love** your neighbor as yourself. (*"And you shall love the Lord your God with all your heart, with all your soul, with all your mind, and with all your strength. This is the first commandment. And the second, like it, is this: You shall love your neighbor as yourself..."*) Maybe you can really relate to where I was when I seemingly *stumbled* across this verse one day. I mean, really, how could I **love** the Lord my God with all my heart, soul and mind? And then there's that whole **love** your neighbor as yourself commandment. This was too much. In fact, in my mind and in the condition I was in when I saw that verse, well, to be blunt, it seemed almost impossible. My heart, soul, and mind were so damaged from the emotional abandonment and sexual abuse, and because in my view *I wasn't enough*, how could I ever have any access to the Lord my God again? And then because I absolutely did not yet **love** myself on any level whatsoever, there was therefore no hope that I could see a way to ever **love** my neighbor. While my mind told me these were impossible commandments to attain, somewhere in the oh-so-damaged recesses of my heart there always remained a *flicker of hope* that maybe, just maybe, there would come a day when I could actually fall in **love** with God; that I could **love** my neighbors, and I could **love** myself. (Years later as Lori and I would journey through our own *stuff*, she was the one who really taught me about love, what it is and what it is not.)

And that's what I want you to consider for yourself. In spite of the circumstances that have brought us together right now and despite the damaged condition in which you may presently find your heart, my prayer for you right here, right now, is that you will cling to whatever ray of hope that might be softly illuminating from the deepest, darkest places known only to you and to the God who created you. As you do, make the *choice* to not give up on the love of God. Why? Because according to the first three words of 1 Corinthians 13:8, *"Love never fails."*

During those times when I had only fragments of splintered hope to grab on to, I would like to be able to share with you that my heart was instantly healed, the generational curse was obliterated, and my life immediately got on track. But that did not happen. It didn't occur because God wasn't fully capable and willing to touch my life, He was. It didn't happen because I wasn't yet willing to *let go and let God*. Let go of what? Control. I was still so terribly self-reliant and selfish. I continued wanting what I wanted, when I wanted it, and really didn't give much consideration to the consequences of my choices. Remember what we shared earlier about our choices? *The choices you and I make today create the circumstances that we then live tomorrow.*

Because of my choices, the next years of my life led me into and out of more unhealthy relationships. Pride continued to be my calling card; and even though I attended college classes, they did not hold my attention. In my pursuit of a then life-long dream of a career in politics, I became the youngest political staffer for a state-wide campaign in Tennessee. But you know what? Nothing I accomplished, no amount of press coverage (being the youngest, I was given a lot of attention), and no one could satisfy me. I could not find peace, nor could my heart attain any lasting contentment. Despite money, some level of personal recognition, and great-looking girlfriends, I was miserable. There's a couple of primary reasons for this misery, and it's found in the Bible where we're reminded of two truths:

God will share His glory with no man.

(*"I am the Lord, that is My name; and My glory I will not give another ..."* Isaiah 42:8)

And

We can gain the whole world and still lose our soul.

(*"For what profit is it to a man if he gains the whole world, and loses his own soul?"* Matthew 16:26)

You see, God loves us too much to sit back and allow our ego to destroy our life. At the same time, though, He loves us enough to allow us to choose how we're going to live and whom we're going to serve. I've learned that He has no problem with you and me having stuff (money, cars, homes, etc.) as long as the stuff doesn't have, doesn't *define* us. You see, Jesus wants to be, He longs to be, both Lord and Savior of our lives. But more on that a little later.

Unbeknownst to me, while all that was going on in my heart and mind, I was on a scheduled spiritual collision course with those two truths mentioned above (*God will share His glory with no man*, and, *we can gain the whole world and still lose our soul.*). By the time I was twenty-one, some six years after the sexual abuse, I still had not yet shared about the abuse with anyone and my desire to remain in politics had waned, but a new professional passion had surfaced: real estate development. The Lord graciously opened a door for me to begin working for and alongside a real estate developer named Terry Parks. It was in the early days of working for Mr. Parks' company, one that developed shopping centers up and down the eastern seaboard of the United States, I slowly began to realize that for some time I had been living with an undeniable sense of fear, a very specific fear that my mom was going to die before she and I reconciled. This fear was real, and it assaulted my mind. I would later discover that fear was the driving force of the generational curse. To understand this is to understand and accept as true that everything planned, every assignment of the devil is fueled by fear. Period. God is the God of faith, and the devil is the creator of fear.

Because I was no longer traveling on the road in politics every day and was instead working in an office, my mind began to slow down long enough for me to realize and acknowledge that for at least the previous four years, this fear had seized my heart and mind. It did what fear is designed to do: it tormented me. (*There is no fear in love; but perfect love casts out fear, because fear involves torment.*" 1 John 4:18) As I purposefully took the time to look back over those four years, I recognized and acknowledged to myself that every single time my phone rang, I immediately tensed up and dreaded answering the call for fear that whomever was on the other end of that line would tell me that mom was no longer with us.

At the end of those four tumultuous and anxiety-ridden years, one March afternoon while working for Mr. Parks, I could relate to what a guy named Job in the Bible experienced when he said in Job 3:25, *"For the thing I greatly feared has come upon me, and what I dreaded has happened to me."* On this particular day, the Spirit of God spoke to me and said, "Call mom."

CALL MOM

Have you ever tried to fill a void on the inside, and no matter what you tried, nothing worked? If you've experienced this, then you'll better understand what I'm about to share.

At twenty-one years old, maybe to an outsider looking in, it seemed as if I had the world by the tail. While working for Mr. Parks' company, I was making a weekly salary, flying around on the company's Lear Jet, continued dating great-looking girls, stayed at the corporately owned condo on the beach in Florida, still doing whatever I wanted, whenever I wanted; and yet, something was off.

Something was really off.

Nothing fulfilled me. Nothing filled the void, a void that I'd later recognize is wholly reserved for the Spirit of God. That void is in every human on the planet today; and just as was the case in my life, the void in every heart of every human will never be fully and joyfully occupied until it is done so by having a personal relationship in your heart, not your mind, with Jesus.

At twenty-one years of age, my emotions were dangerously out of check. The arrogance with which I lived life was rampant. My lifestyle of lying remained in an out-of-control tailspin. The fear of getting hurt was my constant, present companion. The anxiety of daily wondering if today would be *the day* that mom would die was taking a serious emotional toll on me. My unwillingness to bow my heart in humble submission, making the choice to give Jesus control of my life, was becoming too much for me to ignore any longer. I was such a big mess.

And so, on an early March morning, with a lot of anger raging in my heart, anger that was the result of the pain with which I lived life, and with absolutely no humility, I went to the Lord and said, "I'm in church every time the doors are open. I went to Christian schools. All of my friends are Christians. But you know what? I don't believe You are real; I don't think You hear anything I'm saying; and I feel pretty stupid talking to the wind. But, if by some chance, I'm wrong and You really do exist and really do have a plan for my life, PROVE IT!"

Let me quickly share with you a bit of counsel that can be of beneficial service to you for the remainder of your life: do not ever, under any circumstances, ask God, the Creator of the universe, to prove to you that He is real until and unless you are ready for a close encounter of the first kind. When invited to do so, He will invade your life like none other.

Just about as quickly as I prayed that "prove it" prayer, I was on to the next thing, leaving behind any lasting hope that He'd actually respond to my words. To be blunt, my prayer was offered with zero faith. Sometimes, though, because He's such a good God and loves us so very much, He just totally circumvents our unbelief and does that which only He can do. Here's what happened.

About two and a half weeks after I prayed and asked God to prove to me that He is real, I arrived back at our office after having a later than usual lunch break. On that gorgeous March afternoon there wasn't a cloud in the sky, but I remember that it was really windy outside. Walking into our suite of plush and well-decorated offices, I spoke to our receptionist, Sharon; walked down a hallway, turned right, and then another right turn landed me in my office. I shut the door behind me, sat down, and began dialing the phone to check on a situation that needed our attention at a shopping center our firm had just built in Beckley, West Virginia.

While dialing the phone, off behind me and to the left and with no warning whatsoever, I heard a voice clearly and calmly instruct me to, "**Call mom.**" The instruction was so audible that I twirled around in my chair to see who was with me in that office. To my dismay, I saw no one, but clearly, I had just heard a distinct audible instruction.

Not taking any time in trying to figure out what was happening, I instead just did what I had been instructed to do. I called mom. When I did, the phone rang six and then seven times. On the eighth ring, my mom answered the phone, and it was immediately unmistakable that something was terribly wrong. Her voice was slurred, and she sounded totally disoriented. I soon realized that at the precise moment God, by His Spirit, showed up in my office and instructed me to "Call mom," **my mom was attempting suicide.** She was dying, and I could surely hear the life leaving her body. This was the day and the moment that I had been dreading, fearing, for so many years. It was now here. It was happening. Mom was dying.

In moments like that, I don't think that most of us consciously take the time to think or even respond. Instead, many of us just react. And that's exactly what I did. I reactively ran out of my office, down that hallway, blew past Sharon, jumped in my car, and drove at an excessive speed to a little community called Ooltewah, Tennessee, where my parents lived at that time. As I was driving up Interstate 75, I suddenly had a leading to pray – to just talk with this God whom I clearly did not know. I knew the power of prayer, but I did not yet know His love. At this point, I had made Jesus my Savior but not yet my Lord.

At that moment, for the first time in many years, I tried something new for me – I tried being honest. No pretense, no big story, no fantasy world, no lies. I just had a moment where I, with almost no faith, reached out to the Lord and asked Him to please help my mom. In spite of all that we had been through and the fragility of our relationship; as her son, I sure did not want my mom to die. Deep down, I still yearned to be her boy and desperately needed her to love and *accept* me.

As quickly as I began to pray, He responded. In fact, as I prayed, I found myself confessing verse after verse from the Word of God. As a child at Ridgedale Baptist Church in Chattanooga, Tennessee, a lady named Dillie Jenkins had said to me one Sunday morning that she saw something in me and believed that one day God was going to use me to reach a lot of people for Him. Mrs. Jenkins also believed that she was supposed to help encourage me to learn Bible verses. So, for every verse that I memorized, she gave me ten dollars." (Even as a child I enjoyed what money could provide, so I memorized a lot of verses.) All of those years later, while driving to reach my mom, the seed of the Word of God that Mrs. Jenkins had sown into my heart was now producing a harvest on an Interstate in Tennessee.

When I arrived into my parents' neighborhood and drove into their driveway, everything looked fine. From the outside-in, their home was probably much like where you live today. From the inside-out, however, the situation was much different. My mom was dying.

Through the decades of ministering in high schools, I've literally spoken with millions of students and you know what? When I look at these teens from the outside-in, almost always everything looks fine. But if you and I were able to get a different view of their lives, a perspective from the inside-out, I imagine that many of these precious teenagers are in their very own, very personal war; one that is being waged in their hearts and minds, and one that very may well be the result of a generational curse active in them. Maybe today you, too, can relate.

As I slammed my car into park in mom and dad's driveway, I jumped out of it and ran to the front door of their home. Their front door was locked; and because I had not been given a key to their home, my only option was to knock out a window and climb through it. Before doing that, however, I continued knocking; and after waiting for what seemed like an eternity, mom made her way down a flight of stairs, unlocked the door, and fell into my arms. I picked her up, carried her to her car, and drove her back down Interstate 75 to Parkridge Hospital in Chattanooga, Tennessee. (Remember that Parkridge Hospital is the same hospital mom and dad took me to when I was a student at the prep school.)

As we drove to the hospital that afternoon, mom looked over at me and said, "I can't be dying." My response was immediate, "You're not going to die mom, but you're going to have to choose to live." "Choose" is by far the most important word in that last sentence because as we said earlier, *the choices you and I make today create the circumstances that we then live tomorrow.*

Upon arriving at the hospital, we were met at the front door by nurses and an Emergency Room doctor. I vividly remember being shoved against a wall so that mom could then be rushed into the emergency room.

By this point my dad and family friends were already at the hospital, and together we waited for about forty-five minutes with no word from anyone inside the ER. During that time, I felt so alone. Sure, I knew everyone who was there, and they knew me; but because years earlier I had made the decision to not allow anyone into my heart, no intimacy in my life whatsoever, I lived a very public life in a very lonely way. Have you ever felt like even though you were surrounded by lots of people who knew your name, you still felt disconnected and all alone? If so, then you know exactly how I felt.

At the end of those forty-five minutes, that same doctor whom I saw when we arrived walked directly over to my dad and delivered a message that I will never forget. That doctor looked at my dad and said, "Mr. Sikes, I have no medical reason whatsoever to share with you what I'm about to share. All I can tell you is that this is a **miracle of God**. Your wife is alive, she's fine, and you can go see her." And with that report, the doctor, somewhat bewildered himself, turned and walked away.

My dad looked at me and asked if I wanted to go see my mom. I wasn't quite ready to walk into her ER room; so, instead, I let him know that I'd be back in a few minutes – I just needed to take a walk.

MIRACLE OF GOD???? ARE YOU KIDDING ME????
Those were the two thoughts that were chasing each other round-and-round inside my mind. That medical doctor, a man who had four years of college, four years of med school, at least two years of residency, and however many years of practice, just told my dad that medicine had not saved my mom's life. GOD DID.

After taking a short walk by myself, I suddenly felt very drained from the emotional roller coaster we had all been on that gorgeous, windy March afternoon. Several hours had come and gone since I had walked into my office from a late lunch and had driven my mom to a hospital as she was dying. Now, leaning against a long corridor inside Parkridge Hospital, all alone in that hallway, all I can tell you is what happened. I hope you believe me; but whether you do or not, it really happened and it's your *choice* to believe what you're about to read.

I had an encounter with Jesus. Not a religion and not a denominational doctrine. I came face-to-face with a Person, the Son of the living God. His presence was undeniable and standing there, I remember saying, "You're real. You really do exist." As soon as those words left my lips, I suddenly felt a warm and refreshing oil-like substance on top of my head, and it was slowly flowing down my body – from the inside-out. Standing there all-alone with tears welling up in my eyes, I became very aware that all the anger, pain, disappointment, and yes, feeling that *I wasn't enough* with which I had lived since I was four years old, were all colliding, in real time, with the BLESSING of the Lord; with Love Himself.

No doubt, Jesus was in that hallway with me and for the first time since I had become a Christian at seven years old, I genuinely felt His presence show up in my life. In the holiness and total quietness of that moment, somewhere deep in my heart, a heart that was so ravaged with pain, somehow, I knew that God was real, and it had been His Spirit who had instructed me to call mom earlier that afternoon. He and He alone was the reason she was alive.

Then that same voice that I had heard in my office earlier that afternoon again spoke up on the inside of me and said, "I've got something I need you to do for Me. There are generations of teenagers whom I am calling you to reach for Me. These young people have no idea that I'm alive, that I love them, and that I have a plan for their lives. Like you, they live with intense pain. I am going to heal your heart, and then I want you to go on the road and give them My hope. I've called you to minister to teenagers."

I spoke right back to the Him and reminded Him that I had always been behind the scenes, working as someone else's *right-hand* person. I had no desire to be out front and certainly had no desire to be a speaker. Funny thing about the Lord – He doesn't change (*"For I am the Lord, I do not change ..."* Malachi 3:6). I reminded Him that during high school at Boyd-Buchanan I had taken one half of one semester of Public Speaking and how much I had detested every minute of that class. And besides, in my mind, I wasn't a good speaker. Surely, He had something else I could do for Him.

As that afternoon turned into night and then into morning, my mom was released from Parkridge Hospital. Shortly thereafter, she began to get healthier, she went back to school, became a Christian Counselor, and for many, many years, effectively helped people come through challenging seasons of life.

While I could not shake the instruction the Lord had given me in the corridor of that hospital, I continued making my argument to the Him as to why I was not the right guy. How could I conceivably work for Him? After all, I knew nothing about ministry, and for that matter, I knew no one in ministry except for a handful of pastors and youth pastors who worked in churches. But working in a church was not the assignment He had given me in that hospital corridor. He had told me that I was to travel and minister to teenagers. I was very perplexed and saw no way whatsoever of how I was supposed to move out of real estate development into fulltime ministry. But once again, if this transition was ever going to happen, I was becoming acutely aware that it would come down to my trusting Him and not my abilities. It's the same with you, too. Maybe today you are in the midst of a transition. If so, take it from me. Trust the One who is worthy to be trusted. He's got this!!

About six months after that fateful March afternoon at the hospital with my mom, there came a morning that would become another defining moment in my life. It was a moment that would lead me directly into the next season of my journey of faith. Here's what happened.

As was my standard operating procedure, I arrived every morning at our development offices before the sun rose from the eastern sky. And every morning, there was only one car in the parking lot when I arrived; and this, too, was normal. The car belonged to Mr. Terry Parks. As I parked my car and walked past his, I wondered how many hours ago he had arrived at work that morning. I unlocked the front door and took my usual path down the hallway, turned right, and entered my office. When I did, this morning I saw a yellow sticky note in the center of my desk. On it were written three words: Come see me. And it was signed TSP (Mr. Parks). I walked down the hallway and entered the Executive Suite, knocked on Mr. Parks closed office door, and when he invited me in, he asked me to sit down.

Mr. Parks then began to talk with me about his son, Bart, and asked if I could get a demo tape of Bart playing the trumpet into the hands of a Christian musician named Phil Driscoll. I immediately said yes, took the cassette tape from Mr. Parks, and confidently told him I'd be back in touch once I had delivered the demo tape to Mr. Driscoll. With that being settled, our meeting was over, and I excused myself. As I walked back to my office, the two questions on my mind were, "Who is Phil Driscoll?" And, "How do I find him?"

After a quick search, I discovered to my astonishment that Phil Driscoll and his ministry were headquartered thirty minutes north of where I was seated. The more I read about Phil and his accomplishments, the more I understood why Mr. Parks had requested I get Bart's trumpet demo into his hands. Phil is arguably the best trumpet player in the world. And so, that morning I called Phil's office and requested a meeting with him. That request was initially denied, because he was on the road; but if I wanted to come up to his ministry location, it could be arranged for me to meet with Phil's Executive Director, a man named Gregory Pope. Little did I know it that morning, but by sending me to Cleveland, Tennessee, to meet Gregory and see the world headquarters of Phil Driscoll and his evangelistic ministry, the Holy Spirit was leading me right into the perfect will of God for my life. It's no different for you. Here's what I mean. His ways are higher than ours and His thoughts are also higher than ours. He actually sees the end from the beginning; and because His viewpoint is so much grander than yours and mine, our trusting in and surrendering to Him and His guidance are paramount to our successfully living a life of faith.

After meeting Gregory and other members of Phil's staff on that day, he walked me out to my car, and before I left, invited me to come back up to Cleveland in two weeks to sit down and talk with him and Phil. I agreed to do so and two weeks later, I was back in Cleveland. This time, however, I was invited to meet at the Driscoll home. Sitting downstairs with Phil and Gregory, my heart was full of excitement. Though I had now only met Gregory for the second time and was meeting Phil for the first time and even though I really knew nothing about ministry, especially a traveling ministry that invested over 240 days every year on the road, I knew in my heart that I was coming to work for Phil Driscoll Ministries. It wasn't a question of if, it was only a question of when.

Weeks later, through a set of circumstances that no one saw coming, I got a phone call from Gregory Pope and was offered the position of Road Manager for Phil's ministry. I prayed and then went to talk with Mr. Parks. I thanked him for all that he had taught me, for all that he had allowed me to do for his company, and for all of the experiences he had allowed me to be part of. While I was thankful for the past, my future was going to be in ministry and to this end, it was time for me to leave. I had to obey the Lord. Two weeks later, I was working in full time ministry, traveling the world with Phil as his Road Manager. For the next three and a half years, I learned all aspects of a traveling ministry as I was serving Phil and his ministry. Little did I know it then, but every day during those three and a half years while managing over six hundred and fifty ministry events, the Lord was simultaneously teaching and preparing me for a day that was soon approaching.

In June of 1992, the Lord again reminded me of His direction to me as I had stood in the corridor of Parkridge Hospital years ago. I knew in my heart then that it was time to leave Phil's ministry and launch my own ministry that would focus on bringing faith-based *words of hope* to teenagers in high schools, but I did not want to do it. Knowing that now was the time for me to move was apparent, but I loved Phil, his family, and our ministry team and really didn't want to leave.

Have you ever experienced something that you were being led to do, but what you were being led to do was not what you wanted? If your answer is *yes*, then you again know where I was and how I felt. I went to the Lord and asked Him, I begged Him to please change His mind; to please let me stay and continue working with and for Phil.

Well, He didn't change His mind; and in December of 1992, I followed what He had been leading me to do. I went over to the Driscoll home and with tears in my eyes I shared with Phil that the Lord had led me to resign from his ministry and start my own, an outreach to teenagers in high schools.

Ten days later, on Friday, January 1st, 1993, with less than four hundred dollars in the bank, with nothing on my schedule, and no corporate sponsorships, I just did my best to obey the Lord and took the then largest step of faith in my life and created our Spirit of America Foundation. Our ministry was then, and today continues to be, a ministry that is solely dedicated to ministering faith-based *words of hope*, words that boldly declare to teenagers across America and in nations of the world that God loves you; that He has a plan for your life; and that in Him, YOU MATTER. Three years into this journey, however, I was really struggling with being a minister. Being a speaker was one thing; a minister was something totally different. But as He always does, the Lord confirmed to me that we were on the right track as a minister, and He did so through a six-year-old boy at a Shoney's Restaurant in Daytona Beach, Florida.

I had just arrived in Florida to speak at a very small youth event the next day. I didn't want to be there, and honestly, I wasn't in the best of moods when this family picked me up at the airport. My night went from bad to unbearable when we sat down for dinner and this little boy repeatedly asked me over and over the same question, *"Preacher Dean, what are you going to preach on tomorrow?"* Preacher Dean? Where did that come from? I was a speaker, not a preacher. Why didn't this little boy get it right? After asking me for the fourth time what I was going to preach on the next morning, I wanted to reply, "Raising the dead, if you keep asking me about preaching!"

Let's take a brief detour for a quick minute; and as we do, allow me to offer you something to consider in your own life.

In all my time of working in politics, real estate development and then the years I had devoted to working with Phil and his ministry, the one thing that I never did take the time to invest in was me working on me. My heart was so shut down and pride was still so very present. My emotions were frayed and I, either consciously or sub-consciously, was not letting anyone, anywhere close to my heart. In an attempt to protect myself from any and all pain and disappointment, I would not let anyone into a relationship with the real me. I was too afraid of getting hurt. The generational curse was still hanging on and unbeknownst to me, I was allowing it. Don't miss what I just said … I was allowing it.

You see, even if you find yourself working in full time ministry and doing much good for others, the work and the accolades from it will never heal what's broken if you and I do not take time with Him for our own lives and for our own wellness. In fact, it can inflict further and deeper damage. And to be totally transparent with you, working in ministry will never replace you and I just hanging out with Jesus, ministering to Him.

Ok; back to the six-year-old boy and my ministry trip to Florida.

Instead of talking to this young man in response to my preaching subject the next morning about "raising the dead", I offered this little boy an answer that seemed to satisfy his insatiable curiosity and at the same time, somewhere deep in my damaged heart, I knew that out of the mouth of babes, the Lord was inviting me to say yes to the call.

PART FOUR

THE ACCEPTANCE

SAYING YES TO THE CALL

The next morning, I woke up very early with the Florida sunshine blasting through my hotel room window. I was thinking about that little boy form the night before and his question that just refused to make its exodus from my mind, "Preacher Dean, what are you going to preach on tomorrow?" I've learned that God loves you and me so much that He is unwavering in His pursuit of our heart. When He has something He wants to get to you or from you, He is relentless in His quest.

As I left my hotel and walked across the street to the event where a stage and sound system had been assembled earlier that Saturday morning, I did so wondering why I was even there. After all, I spoke in high schools and this event was promoted as an evangelistic meeting. I wasn't an evangelist; I was a motivational speaker. In fact, for the first several years of our ministry, I refused to call myself a minister. I was instead a motivational speaker and when that title no longer satisfied my heart, I became an inspirational speaker, reasoning within myself that it was the Lord who *inspired* the words I spoke.

Quick side note: If ever you find yourself in a wrestling match between your will and the will of the Father, do yourself a favor and quickly say *yes* to Him. Oh, how I wish I had taken that advice myself, but it would be several frustrating years before I would eventually say *yes* to His call. In fact, my experience was much like Jonah in the Bible. When the Lord gave me clear instructions to pursue our own ministry in January of 1993, I continued to be self-reliant and did so on my own terms, not His. That choice sent me on a journey which eventually led me right back to His original plans and purposes for our life and ministry.

Now, back to that Saturday morning event. As I arrived beside the stage, suddenly what I now know to have been anxiety, vehemently and relentlessly beat against my heart and mind. The devil was doing everything within his power to stop this morning from happening. As was his standard operating procedure, he caused me to once again wrestle with more questions, questions that were yet again fruit from the root of the generational curse that had been part of my life for so very long. Questions like:

"It's one thing to be a speaker; what makes you think you're qualified to be a minister?

What do *you* have to say?

What will you do if no one responds to your words?

You don't have what it takes. Don't you remember? *You're not enough.*

With those questions and thoughts assaulting my mind, I was introduced, and the service began. When I'm introduced as a speaker in high schools, there's usually anywhere between five hundred and fifteen hundred students who are staring at me. On this day, however, there were no more than **twenty** people at this event; quite a break from our norm relating to the size of the crowd. While my mind struggled, the anointing of God showed up, and my heart became oh so peaceful. The anointing is, in the simplest of terms, the manifested presence and power of God. Then it happened. When I finished sharing my testimony, I gave an altar call, an invitation, for anyone there to receive Jesus as Lord of his or her life. After a minute or so of waiting, a young man slowly walked out from under some overarching trees that offered some much-needed shade from the blistering Florida sunshine. As he stood at the base of that stage, the Lord gave me the honor of leading him into a personal relationship with Jesus. As I walked off that stage and was driven back to the airport, the anointing was still very much present and the smile on my face would have been impossible to miss. I now knew that I was where He wanted me to be.

For the next ten years, I enthusiastically pursued the evangelistic calling to minister our prophetic *message of hope* to teenagers across America and in other nations of the world. We reached one hundred thousand students each year. I was so grateful to have such a full schedule and even more thankful to see how the Lord was constantly using our ministry to touch the lives of teens around the world. Even so, I was still living a very public life in a very private and lonely way.

Of all the people I encountered all over the world, I reasoned that surely one of them would be my wife, the person with whom I could spend my life, but my meeting someone by happenstance was not how she and I were going to meet. You see, I was once again so busy with the reigns of my life tightly wound around my own hands, trying to make relationships happen in my own ability, rather than leaning instead on the One who knew not only who the lady was He had chosen for me but also knew where she was. The stubbornness caused by my self-reliance was completely preventing me from experiencing God's best. That's the thing about the sin of self-reliance; it keeps us from the very desires of our heart. At thirty years of age, I was so lonely. Maybe you can relate to how I was feeling. You see, for years the generational curse constantly told me that *I wasn't enough.* But in the summer of 1995, my life was about to change.

In July and August of 1995, I encountered the mercy of God, The GRACE LIFE we talked about earlier. In His mercy, the key turning point to my meeting the lady God had chosen for me happened when I called a friend of mine named David Young. Here's some of what transpired on that phone call.

It had been an unusually long trip on the road; and when I got back home, I was really tired. But more than being tired from the trip, I was so tired of being alone. I remember tossing my luggage and briefcase over into a corner, walking into my office, picking up the phone, and calling David. As quickly as he answered the phone and said, "Hello," I unleashed my frustration. I went on and on and on about all that I was *doing* for God, and all I really wanted Him to do for me was bring the lady who would become my wife into my life. I reasoned to David, "After all, there are billions of people alive in the earth today. I'm asking for one. Is that too much to ask?"

Hearing the frustration in my voice, David laughed at me. He actually laughed and then very seriously said, "Shut up. Stop asking. Begin thanking."

He then imparted a life lesson to me when he explained that everytime I asked God where my wife was, I was in fact sowing a *seed of doubt*. Remember that according to Genesis 8:22, *"While the earth remains, seedtime and harvest, cold and heat, winter and summer, and day and night SHALL NOT CEASE."* In other words, everything in the Kingdom of God is the result of seedtime and harvest. David then told me to change my words and as an act of faith begin thanking the Lord for my wife (seed); *thanking Him in advance* for that which I desired (harvest). In spiritual terms, David was telling me to live by faith, not by sight.

He even went so far as to suggest that I write down on paper a list of the attributes that I desired in a wife and to do so very specifically. Well, none of what David was instructing and suggesting made any sense to my mind, but man it sure made sense to my heart. After all, I had tried for years to find my wife on my own, and that surely hadn't worked. Like everything else that the Lord was teaching me during this season of my life, meeting the lady who would become my wife was going to be an act of faith. My part was to get out of the way, to let go and let God, and most of all, take my trust off of my ability and put my trust completely in and on Him.

I thanked David for being so bold and blunt with me, hung up the phone, and got a piece of paper and a pen. I reasoned, "Why put off until tomorrow that which I can do today?" And so, I prayed and asked the Holy Spirit to help me put on paper what He wanted me to believe for in the person He had selected for me to do life with. As soon as I asked, He answered. Within minutes, I had my list. And it wasn't just a list of spiritual attributes. I was led to also include her physical look and her personality. You see, I was learning that God is in the details; and as we delight ourselves in His Word, He in turn loves to give to us the desires of our heart.

At the end of each day for the next forty-five days or so, I'd be led to go for a walk where I'd raise my hands and thank God for this lady that was on my list. Why would I raise my hands? Great question. No matter what country I have ever ministered in, universally, hands raised is a sign of surrender. And so, as I went on those nightly walks with hands raised and words of thanksgiving coming out of my heart through my lips, I was daily surrendering my search for my wife to the Lord. As I did, my confession of faith would once again become *not my will but yours*. I thanked the Lord for my wife's health, for her safety, but most of all, I thanked Him that she and I were one day closer to meeting and beginning our life together.

Then, on a Sunday morning in August of 1995, Lori Turner walked into our church. I *just happened* to be in town that weekend and was sitting near the back of the auditorium when she walked in through the back door. As she walked past me, I heard myself saying, "That's my list. That's her." The Bible teaches us in Proverbs 18:22 that, *"He who finds a wife, finds a good thing and obtains favor from the Lord."* The instant I saw Lori I knew she was to be my wife. You see, in all of those walks with the Lord, in all those moments of honest surrender, I was *finding* Lori in the realm of the Spirit. So, when I saw her that Sunday morning with my *natural* eyes, my *spiritual* eyes knew that she was the one. I had *found* her in the spiritual world. Remember earlier how we talked about there being a spiritual world that is more real and more active than the natural world in which you and I live? This is what I'm talking about right now; and so we don't forget, I'm led to once again remind you that everything that happens in the natural world first begins in the spiritual world.

During a two-minute meet-and-greet that Sunday morning before the pastor began to minister, I walked up to the front of that auditorium where Lori was seated with her parents. To my dismay,

81

Lori's dad turned around, grabbed my arm, and said, "I want you to meet my daughter." I was like, "Dear Lord in heaven; yes, Sir. I want to meet your daughter!!" Lori and I said hello to one another; and with that the meet and greet came to an end, and I returned to my seat.

I have absolutely no idea what the pastor said that Sunday morning, but what I did know was God was moving on my behalf. The next week I called Lori and asked if we could have lunch. I picked her up on a Thursday afternoon and went to an outdoor café in Chattanooga. I didn't even taste the food I ate but was instead mesmerized by this young lady. I hung onto every word she spoke, and what seemed like only minutes had turned into an hour and it was time to take Lori back to her work.

After dropping her off, I called my sister, Deanna, and said, "I've just had lunch with the girl I'm going to marry." Sure enough, Lori and I met in August of 1995, thirty-seven days later in September we were engaged, and on May 4th, 1996, we were married. Ten days later Lori was pregnant; and for the next three years, our family grew and grew and grew as our son, Will, was born in 1997, our oldest daughter, Ellie, was born in 1998 and our youngest daughter, Meg, was born in 1999. At one point, Lori and I had all three of our children in diapers! As we look back over those first five years of marriage, we oftentimes truly wonder how the Lord kept everything going.

As Lori and I worked together in raising our family and I continued traveling with our ministry, several things became oh so clear to me relating to her: Lori was my best friend; she is the best mom I've ever known; and she is a person of great faith. Even with all that God was doing in our family and through our ministry, I was still broken on the inside. Everywhere I went and no matter what success we enjoyed, there remained that nagging, deep, dark statement looming in my heart – I still believed that *I wasn't enough.* And let me again share with you why I continued to do so. When you and I have not dealt with the core issue, whatever that core issue might be, it continues to operate. Nothing

I accomplished and nothing I had would ever *be enough* as long as the generational curse of ***I'm not enough*** was present and active in my life.

That said, never underestimate the power of a praying spouse. In Lori, God gave me the person in whom I could fully trust, and trust was what I was about to really need. You see, with the busyness of life and a fulltime ministry schedule, I still had not yet taken the time to deal with my emotions; specifically, the aftermath of having been emotionally abandoned and then sexually abused over two decades earlier. I had not yet dealt with my emotions and they were now dealing with me. Here's what I was about to better understand: *hurting people oftentimes hurt people.* In my case, my words were hurting my wife. Five years into our marriage, Lori, the person in whom I had fallen so deeply in love, told me that I was mean and to not come home until I got some help.

DON'T COME HOME UNTIL YOU GET SOME HELP

It was 9:30 am on Friday, May 4th, 2001, when I excitedly called Lori from the road and shared that I had a surprise for her for on our fifth-year wedding anniversary. We were going back to the very place we had spent our honeymoon. Everything was set: kids were taken care of, the trip was paid in full, and all she needed to do was pack a bag.

When I got home later that afternoon, we could take off for the beach.

I never saw her response coming. She very calmly said, "Dean, I love you, and I want us to last. But Dean, you're mean, and your words really hurt me. I'm not going anywhere with you this weekend; in fact, I don't want you to come home until you get some help." And with that, she hung up the phone. I was dumbfounded. I called her back, but she sent me to voicemail.

I slid down in my car feeling more rejected than at any other time that I could remember in my life. In actuality, I had not heard what Lori had said. Instead, with her hanging up on me and not answering my follow-up call, I was immediately back to being four years old in that hospital room watching my mom hold my sister. I was back at six years old singing for a lady who had no response to my performance. I was back at the prep school where I had been bullied. The scroll was rolling and the message I was hearing was clear … *I wasn't enough.*

I was so angry and at the same time, so hurt. I called my best friend, Gregory Pope (the same Gregory Pope who had hired me at Phil Driscoll's ministry) who now pastors a church in South Georgia and shared with him what had just happened. He insisted that I leave right then, come to his home for the weekend, and to talk with a friend of his who was also in town over the weekend. Little did I know it then, but in my going to Douglas that day God was setting me up to talk with a professional Counselor who specialized in overcoming emotional abandonment and sexual abuse.

Within minutes of hanging up with Gregory, instead of heading to the beach with my wife, I called Lori and shared with her that I was driving 323 miles south on I-75 to South Georgia. When I arrived at Pope's home, I was tired but as an alternative to calling it a night and going to bed, it was suggested that we immediately hop back in the car and go sit down with this friend who was a Counselor. I reluctantly agreed to do so. When we arrived at this meeting, I had minimal expectation that counseling would work for me. We nonetheless sat down, and this gentleman asked me one question. His question unlocked a portion of my heart and I talked for the next three hours. After this, it was really late into the night, so I went to bed. This Counselor and I agreed that we'd meet again the next morning at 9 am where we could talk a bit more. Morning came quickly; and this time, when we sat down, he asked me two questions, and our conversation lasted about 90 minutes. Those two sessions proved to be both timely and so very helpful to me; it was now time to go home to Lori and our kids.

We said our good-byes; and as I drove those 323 miles back to Chattanooga, I cried most of the way. More than once on that drive home, I had to pull off the road to wipe my eyes. Little did I realize it then but in my tears were the beginning of the healing that would forever change the course of our lives and ministry. God was showing me then the importance of dealing with emotions and He was using a Christian Counselor to jumpstart the process. This would not be the last time that He would use counseling to advance the healing of my heart, healing that would prove to be the truest journey of faith I would ever take.

A big part of my recognizing and accepting the importance of trusting the Lord to heal my heart and continuing in Christian-based counseling came weeks later when I walked into a Home Depot with two of our children. Let me be clear. If you and I knew each other, there would be things about you that I do not know as I sit here and type these words. Likewise, because you and I do not know each other, there are things about my life that you do not know. One of the things that you do not yet know is that Home Depot, or for that matter, any store like Home Depot, is not a place that I frequently visit. Not because it's not a great store, it is. It's because home improvement skills do not exist in me. At all.

My walking into a Home Depot with our kids that day was something I had never before done. That being said, you may now better understand why what happened next torpedoed me into a tailspin.

Walking down an aisle, holding Will's hand in my right hand and Ellie's hand in my left, we rounded a corner and I literally walked right into the person who had sexually abused me when I was 15 years old. In that instant, I was immediately back to being fifteen years old, in that bedroom, on that bed. Standing there on aisle 15 at Home Depot, I couldn't speak. Truthfully, my world was unraveling and was doing so at what seemed an unfair and warped speed. We acknowledged each other, and I quickly turned around and as I was holding tighter to both Will and Ellie, the three of us made a direct line for the nearest Exit. I quickly buckled the kids into their car seats and somehow, with my heart racing and my mind reeling, we made it safely back home. Sitting in our driveway I knew in my heart that my life was about to be exposed, and I saw no way of stopping it from happening.

A few hours later, as dinnertime came and went and our kids were now in bed, when I could no longer mask the emotional dam that was clearly breaking, I remember asking Lori to step outside to our front porch with me. After taking a deep breath and asking the Lord to help me do that which I had never before done since it had happened to me, I invited the only person I had ever fully trusted into such a private space of personal pain. Without stopping for even a second, I took this step of faith and trusted both the Lord and Lori, and then shared with her every detail of the abuse.

I had no idea how Lori would either react or respond to what she was being told, but somehow the Lord gave me the assurance to trust her. When I was nearing the end of sharing with her the *headlines* from the past twenty-two years of my life and relating to her that I had run into this person at Home Depot earlier that afternoon, I stopped talking and watched for what would happen next. Lori met my vulnerability with a redeeming love, a welcoming grace, and a fierce compassion.

She looked at me with such care and said, "Dean, now everything makes sense.

We really need to get you some help. I'm here for you and am not going anywhere. I know in my heart that you need to start consistently talking with a counselor, immediately." And so, with Lori as my trusted encourager, even though I was so new to all that Christian counseling had to offer, and truthfully, despite the positive experience I had just had in Douglas, I was terribly uncomfortable in seeing a counselor on a regular basis. My being uncomfortable did not stop me. The next morning I made my appointment and a week later, slowly began the work of becoming healthy, spiritually and emotionally.

For our family, with the generational curse with which I had lived for so long near the point of exposure, the next season of life was a very painful one where the focus was unpacking the pain.

UNPACKING THE PAIN

I remember the very first day I went to counseling. It was both unnerving and frightening, almost beyond description. As I approached the front door to the counselor's office, my heart was racing and the anxiety with which I had learned to live was so very present and almost breathtaking.

You know, the stories we tell ourselves oftentimes far outweigh the reality of what we live; but on this particular day, the reality I was about to walk in to was exactly as I had imagined it would be. I assumed that just on the other side of that big, heavy, wooden, brown door there would be a room full of people who were seated in chairs, all of whom were waiting to sit and share their problems with a professional. There would be men and women, boys and girls, all of us alike in some way.

I reasoned within myself that because I was on television quite often, there was a very good chance that the enemy would make sure that I would be recognized. Once again, I was separating myself from everyone else with that fake air of superiority that was all part of the generational curse. And then, true to form, as had been the case for decades, here came the questions:

How would I explain to anyone who might recognize me why I was there? (By the way, at that point, it never even crossed my mind that no one really cared why I might be in counseling. Pride and arrogance were hanging on for all they were worth.)

What good was Christian counseling even going to do? After all, I reasoned that as a Spirit-filled Believer I certainly knew how to pray and apply the Word so why even go to counseling?

What would I say when I sat down with the counselor?

What if this professional saw through me and she, too, with all of her education, training, and experience, realized that *I wasn't enough*?

At that moment, the generational curse was at war with my mind, but this time I was not going to let it and the pride that came with it stop me. Despite the spiritual warfare that was raging inside me, the Holy Spirit helped me to push through and open the door. I walked in, signed the registration sheet, and then said to the receptionist, "Hi. I'm Dean Sikes, and I'm here for my appointment."

After being handed a stack of papers to fill out, I quickly found a seat in the lobby, near the back of the room, somewhat away from the other clients. I busied myself by burying my head in the paperwork and after returning the completed questionnaire to the front desk, I nervously went back to my seat and sat in quiet obscurity, waiting to hear my name called. It wasn't long before my name echoed throughout the lobby of the counseling office and I stood up and dutifully walked behind the counselor who, after a few seconds of pleasantries, would soon begin asking me questions.

Fifty minutes came and went for me like I was watching paint dry on a wall. I did not enjoy the questions and the probing, but I could not deny that in my open and honest communication with her, I sensed my heart positively responding to the experience.

When that first session came to a conclusion, I stood up and thanked the counselor for her time. I walked back down that long hallway, across the lobby, up to the big, brown, wooden, door, and finally made my exit.

As I sat down in the safety of my car, I could not believe how emotionally exhausted I was. I was used to six-day trips where we'd travel from Tennessee to London, England, I'd minister in the U.K. five or six times in three days, and then fly back to the states. Those trips back and forth across the Atlantic did not bring the exhaustion I was experiencing from the last 50 minutes and what had been unblocked and maybe even unlocked in that short timeframe. If you have been, or are today in therapy, I imagine you can attest to what I was feeling during that entrance into the world of Christian counseling.

Sitting there in my car, I called Lori and we talked very briefly about what had just happened. True to form, Lori didn't push and prod. She gave me the space I needed; and when I was ready, she was sure to be available as I cautiously continued the journey of opening up more and more of my heart to her. Lori was becoming the safest person in my life, and really, isn't that who your spouse is supposed to be?

For the next ten years, I was semi-consistent in going to counseling as I exercised my faith and believed God to put me with the counselor with whom I could truly connect. I needed someone who wasn't impressed with my life, someone who really didn't care who I knew or who knew me. I needed someone who'd just consistently love me back into the direction of health.

It was also during this same time I became aware that Lori was consumed with an addiction of her own, an addiction that, for that season of our lives, was robbing her of the life God wanted her to live. It was an addiction that almost cost everything that Lori held dear, most of which being her family. Living with Lori and this addiction angered me beyond anything I had ever before experienced; and, as I would later discover, it angered me because in my mind, I had made the addiction about me. The generational curse was consistently and relentlessly hard at work. As her husband, because Lori was *choosing* an addiction that caused her to numb out, once again the message my mind was sending me and the message I was willfully buying was, *I'm not enough*. Only this time, it was a message that had Lori and our marriage tied to it. This time, the *I'm not enough* message was going for the knockout punch. This time, the enemy was telling me that *I wasn't enough* for Lori. Otherwise, if I were enough, she wouldn't be giving in to this numbing-out addiction. And so, true to form, like every single time before, here came the questions:

Has Lori been unfaithful?

Does Lori still love me?

Has Lori ever loved me?

Is our marriage going to last?

But most of all, here was the resounding question that refused to go away – Why am *I not enough* for Lori to be happy; why is she choosing to numb out?

Here's the thing about the enemy, and I really hope you let this statement of truth sink in – the devil, one hundred percent of the time, always overplays his hand. He always goes one step too far; and when he does, you and I have the opportunity to say, *"Enough is enough!"* In Jesus' name, *I choose the GRACE LIFE that comes with the BLESSING of the Lord,"* over the generational curses that come with the enemy of your very life. Jesus is the Way Maker and when we turn to Him and say, *not my will but yours,* and we mean it, look out. Something good is coming our way. And for Lori and me, that *something good* was her total and complete deliverance.

The addiction that had such control over her life and the miracle of how the Lord instantaneously set her totally free is Lori's story to tell. Out of respect for my wife, all I will say any more about this addiction in this book is that between the generational curse and all that it brought with it into my life and the addiction and all that it brought with it into Lori's life, we were on a collision course that nothing and no one except Jesus Himself could have salvaged. Remember what we said much earlier in our time together? Healthy attracts healthy and unhealthy attracts unhealthy. At that point and unbeknownst to us, Lori and I had actually been unhealthy attracting unhealthy from our very beginning. But praise God, this was changing. So be encouraged. If today you find yourself in a relationship that is unhealthy, and if you take the time to look at yourself and discover that you, too, are emotionally unhealthy, according to Isaiah 43:16 (*"Thus says,* *the Lord, who **makes a way** in the sea …*") the Lord always makes a way to lead us from where we are to where He wants us to be. His Word is our guide. Our responsibility is to Hear his voice of instruction in the Word and to then obey what we have heard.

Lori and I know firsthand that God has a way of taking broken people who are willing and obedient and then rebuilding their lives. And for us, He jumpstarted us into our healing through the counseling ministry of one of the kindest men I've ever known.

I don't even remember how we met this man, who for the sake of anonymity in this space, will be referred to only as The Doctor. I so vividly remember the very first day he, Lori, and I sat together in his office on the third floor of an office building that ironically was connected to the church where Lori and I were married, a church that Lori and her family attended as she was growing up. Looking back at that location, it has become clearer and clearer to us that the Holy Spirit was taking us back to where we became *one* to offer us a life of healing and freedom.

During that first session together, we were not in his office for more than ten minutes when The Doctor looked at me and then looked at Lori and said, "Lori, would you please excuse us. I need to talk with Dean." I was so excited because in my mind, I surmised that The Doctor had quickly identified the problem and he needed to talk with me about what he and I were going to do to help *fix* Lori. Nothing could have been further from the truth. He looked at me and said, "Dean, Lori is going to be OK. My focus needs to be on you." To say that I was dumbfounded would have been the understatement of all understatements. These were just some of the thoughts that were hitting my brain in supersonic, rapid succession: *Your focus needs to be on me? Are you serious? You can't be serious. That woman that God gave me, she's the problem. Get her back in here.*

The Doctor then let me sit there in my anger and self-imposed silence for some time. He wasn't changing his mind; and if we were going to work together, I would be the one to move in his direction. He wasn't about to budge. After several minutes of uncomfortable silence for me, I asked him what he saw that caused him to so quickly dismiss Lori and instead turn his full attention to me. His response was immediate, and it was purposeful. "Dean, your focus is on Lori, not yourself. Lori's focus was totally on herself and not you. That told me everything I needed to know for now. Do you want to continue our session?

After a few more seconds, I responded in the affirmative and that answer would later prove to be one of the wisest choices I've ever made. I'd soon recognize a lesson that the Lord was teaching me as I sat in that office for those few minutes. It's a lesson that might be helpful to you as you live your life: When faced with two options and you're not quite sure which option to pursue, without any hesitation of contradiction and despite the fear of the unknown, ***pursue the options that requires the most FAITH***. Faith in what, you might be asking. Faith in what the Word of God says about the situation you are facing. Why is faith the correct course to pursue? Because as we see in Hebrews 11:6, "...*without faith it is impossible to please Him* ...", and faith is what will cause you to go on the journey of a lifetime. As a side note please remember that the fear you allow in your life will always contaminate and limit the faith in your life. Fear and faith will never co-exist. So how do we see fear leave our life? Turn over to 1 John 4:18 and see it for yourself: "*There is NO fear in love; but perfect love casts out fear* ..." Get this truth in your heart: ***Perfected love cast out all fear.***

And so, with faith in the Word of God as my strength and freedom my desired destination, The Doctor and I met at least twice each month for the next four years. During those meetings, even as I oftentimes tried to focus on Lori and what she was either doing or not doing, he kept me going in the direction of looking at and working on me. Through the words he spoke and the truth he shared, The Doctor's Christian faith was gently woven into the tapestry that reflected his and my professional relationship. With each of our sessions, his godly counsel was something I more and more embraced in my life; and as I did, I became a student and took page after page of notes. The Holy Spirit reminded me that God had written a book so that you and me and every other human ever born could have a time-tested point of reference that was 100% truth - the truth that we could return to for guidance, correction, and comfort. In the notes I took while listening to and dialoguing with The Doctor, those written reminders would serve and today continue to serve, along with the Word of God, as words of truth that likewise offer me guidance, correction and comfort.

Here's a sampling of some of the one-liners I wrote down during my time with The Doctor; maybe some of these will be helpful to you even now –

Trauma can be a result of what I did not get.

Call my own fouls. (Acknowledge when I miss it.)

Read the book, Boundaries.

An unloving way of speaking the truth is the wrong way of doing it.

Most people don't change because they see the light, they change because they feel the heat.

We are not perfect, but we are redeemed.

Jesus used questions not to get answers, but rather to see what was in the persons' heart.

I want to be quick to call my own fouls; slow to anger; and model humility to our kids.

Don't kill a mosquito with a sledgehammer.

Anxiety is an inability to sit still. It's an inability to slow down and smell the roses. It's an inability to trust. It's always looking ahead with *what if*, and not being able to enjoy the now.

Meditate on God's Word - not just memorizing it.

So many people want a plan to follow rather than a **Person** to trust.

There's an ache inside of me to be affirmed by my family of origin that Lori can never fulfill. Only the Lord can fill this void and take away that pain.

Shame is the fuel of addiction.

The heart of the matter is the matter of the heart.

We must be still before God and be fully present with Him.

Ministry is received, not achieved.

You can't have intimacy without true vulnerability.

It's a tragedy to die young but it's a greater tragedy to grow old and to have never lived.

Forgiveness is choosing how to remember the past in a way that doesn't negatively affect the present and future.

YOUMATTER is an interesting name for our ministry in light of the fact that for my life up until recently, I've struggled with knowing that I matter.

Those are just a handful of the nuggets The Doctor sowed into the soil of my heart as he and I invested years together in the process of my getting better. As my time with him came to a close and our professional relationship ended, Lori and I both sensed that counseling for me was not yet quite over. There was still work that I needed to do. And so, after praying about the next step, the Holy Spirit connected us with a Christian marriage counselor who would prove to be exactly who we needed, when we needed, and for the very reasons we needed her in our lives. Remember, when we come to God in faith and ask for His will, He always answers us. Again, our job is to hear His voice and to then obey what we just heard.

As the Lord used the gift of counseling to help me navigate through some pretty deep waters of emotional damage into one day getting to live life with a care-free heart, He simultaneously was using Galatians 3:13 & 14 to offer me insight into some of what He had wanted me to see for so long. I'd encourage you to consider what you're about to read, not as it relates to my life, but instead, to yours.

*"Christ has redeemed us from the **curse** of the law, having become a curse for us (for it is written, "Cursed is everyone who hangs on a tree"), that the **blessing** of Abraham might come upon the Gentiles in Christ Jesus, that we might receive the promise of the Spirit through **faith**."*

Contained within those two verses of scripture is the truth that I hope you are seeing as you read this book. Take a minute and go back and slowly and on purpose read every word of Galatians 3:13 and 14; and as you do, pay close attention to the first seven words you see – CHRIST HAS REDEEMED US FROM THE CURSE. He's already done the work. Our responsibility is to receive by faith His completed work into our individual lives.

Here's a question that I finally saw. From before I ever took my first breath, what did the enemy see about my life and the calling on it that so scared him that he orchestrated the generational curse that would almost destroy my life and many of the lives of people whom I so dearly love? How about you? What does that same enemy see about your life, your future, that he's doing his best to stop you from living the GRACE LIFE with the BLESSING of the Lord active in your everyday living? As you consider that question, here are a few more thoughts that might be helpful as you dig out your response to each:

Do you recognize what has control over you (recognition is half the battle)?

Is the Word of God your final authority?

Are you embracing and receiving as yours the BLESSING of the Lord?

Are you daily practicing the GRACE LIFE of letting go and letting God?

Do you trust those whom He shows you are safe people in your life?

Are you fearful of being vulnerable?

Ever considered if the Lord desires for you to invest a season of your life in Christian-based Counseling?

For me, I now realize The Doctor and this Christian marriage counselor were truly an answer to prayer. For you see, in what I learned and then applied from sitting in their offices over the years, little did I know it then, but Christian counseling would better prepare me for coming face-to-face with walking with my mom during nine months of Parkinson's Disease.

NINE MONTHS OF PARKINSONS

It was a Thursday morning in May of 2019 when mom and dad, Deanna and I walked into the office of a Neurologist who held in her hands a manila folder filled with a lot of papers. All of these had something to do with the diagnosis mom had recently been given and was now explaining some of why her handwriting was suddenly so difficult to read and why she no longer was walking without the assistance of a walker or a wheelchair. During this particular appointment, I remember experiencing a sinking feeling in my heart as we listened to what the doctor was sharing. As we listened to the report, the Spirit of God spoke up on the inside of me and said, "This is going to be a process, Dean. Get prepared." The news that day from the Neurologist was neither good nor was it, in the natural, promising … at all. And this was only the first of several doctor's appointments mom had over the course of the next couple of days.

Seeing her struggle to get into and out of dad's car as he lovingly took her from office to office and watching as the prescriptions for her new medicines began to dramatically increase in number, helped mom and dad, Deanna and me to better understand and appreciate the battle we were facing. We believed by faith, though, that Jesus had already won this battle by paying the price for mom's healing at the cross.

To be honest, it was very difficult for me to accept the diagnosis along with the prognosis mom had been given. After all, she had always been able to *white-knuckle* her way through anything, not the least of which was living for the past decade with unimaginable back pain as a result of a freakish boating accident that had left her with multiple fractures in her back. Despite the pain, we just always saw mom as a person who put her faith in the Word of God and kept going. Her faith and dependence upon the Lord notwithstanding, our family was about to discover that mom's time on earth was slowly and inevitably coming to an end.

On the night of July 2, 2019, the Holy Spirit spoke to me and said, "What you're doing for your mom isn't working. Get proactive." When I heard what He said, I immediately called Deanna and shared this same Word with her. She agreed that what I had just heard was truly from Him, and we planned to meet at mom and dad's home early the next morning, July 3.

As we walked into their home, the look on dad's face immediately told Deanna and me that something was really wrong. A Home Health Care Nurse was already scheduled to come to their home that morning for her initial visit with mom. Within minutes of our arriving, the Nurse knocked on the door, and dad immediately took her into their bedroom where mom was obviously in serious medical distress.

The nurse took one look and she forewent all customary introductions, and instead focused on mom's vital signs. Her blood pressure was tanking, and her heart rate was slowing. The nurse called mom's doctor and an ambulance was quickly dispatched to their home. Moments later paramedics were kneeling beside mom, working with her; and a few minutes thereafter, we were in cars, following the ambulance to the hospital. Driving to the hospital, the anxiety and fear that I had lived with from the time I was 17 until 21 years old, the anxiety that caused me to then always wonder if the next phone call was the one informing me that mom had just died, came crashing back against my heart and mind. This time, however, I was spiritually stronger and emotionally much healthier. This time, I spoke back to the fear and did so with the authority we have as a Believer, using the Word of God as my weapon. And you know what? As I spoke only the Word, the fear and anxiety stopped. The BLESSING of the Lord was beating the generational curse of fear. What does this have to do with you? Here's something for you to consider: my Spiritual Father taught me something a long, long time ago when he said to me, **"Dean, you and I will never beat thoughts with thoughts. We beat thoughts with WORDS and words in RED always win."** In other words, no matter what comes your way from the enemy, only speak the Word of God (the answer). Remember, the only thing God is honor-bound to respond to is His Word coming out of your mouth, in faith. How do I know this? Jeremiah 1:12 in the Amplified version tells us so: *"Then said the Lord to me, you have seen well, for I am alert and active, watching over My Word to perform it."*

After arriving at the hospital, we were met by a team of emergency room doctors and nurses. One look at mom's vitals and these medical professionals instantly went to work to save her life. Six hours into this ER treatment, I stood with the primary doctor in charge of mom's care. As he and I talked, I let him know that I was scheduled to minister that night at a local church in Chattanooga and unless he told me it was ok to go minister and then return to the hospital, we were going to cancel my being at that service. I then plainly asked him if mom was going to die that night. His response was simply, "Don't go far."

He then shared with Deanna, dad and me that after all of the bloodwork, X-rays and echocardiograms, the team of doctors all confirmed that mom was obviously very, very sick. She was diagnosed with sepsis, pneumonia, and Parkinson's Disease. She would spend the next twenty-four days in two hospitals, being transported from the Emergency Room to a Medical Intensive Care Unit, to a Cardiac Care Unit, to an Intensive Rehabilitation Hospital, then home with 24/7 care. Once she was back home things really got bad; and after two more weeks of trying to manage all of the care that mom needed, both physically and medically, it was clearly apparent to dad, Deanna and me that mom needed advanced care and she needed it now. We visited a highly acclaimed Assisted Living Facility that was within a stone's throw of mom and dad's home; and as God always does, He met the need our family had as an apartment within this facility miraculously opened up and within just a few days, we moved mom to her new home.

As I shared at the beginning of this book, over the next nine months while she was living at this Assisted Living Facility, mom and I had a lot of time together. As we did, the Lord gave me such a depth of compassion for her and the life she had lived. While I did not excuse what had happened, nor did I excuse what should have happened but did not between us for the past fifty years, I have peace in knowing that just as dad and Deanna were there for mom, I, too, was there as we all walked together during her final days here on earth.

Mom wanted to finish her life at her home; and so, in late February of 2020, the Lord led us to move her home from the Assisted Living Facility. Three weeks later, on Friday morning, March 13th, 2020 at 11:25 am, dad, Deanna, Tony (Deanna's husband), two Care-Givers, a Hospice nurse and I stood in mom and dad's bedroom as she was now only minutes away from her departure from this life and her simultaneous entrance into the next. Surrounding her bed, as one of the Caregivers began to sing, we all quietly joined together in singing the song, I CAN ONLY IMAGINE. As we did, at 11:35 am, mom took her last breath here and peacefully slipped away. Standing around her bed, in the deep, deep silence of that moment, the Holy Spirit whispered these words to my heart, *"She no longer has to imagine, your mom is here."* That Word from the Lord brought our family such peace.

This moment and the moments that would soon turn into hours and then days were unlike any I had ever before lived. For this would be the first time in my life that mom was gone. If you have had someone in your life die then I'm sure that you, too, understand in your own way what I was feeling as life without mom began to be our new norm. Standing alone in dad's garage that Friday morning, the Lord again spoke to me; this time He said, "Use this time, Dean, to reset your ministry." A few minutes later

He would say to me, "I want you to minister at your mom's Celebration of Life Service."

Three days later I stood behind mom's casket and ministered at her funeral.

During the days and weeks that would follow, I would look back over that Celebration of Life service and all that the Holy Spirit had taught me over the past year and a half. As I did, He showed me how to reset our ministry to teens and to those who have teenagers in their life. Then He began to show me that now was the time to write the book that I had been afraid to write.

WRITE THE BOOK YOU'VE BEEN AFRAID TO WRITE

As we've shared throughout the pages of this book, I believe that the most important thing you and I will ever do in our life is hear the voice of God. The second most important thing we will ever do is obey what we just heard. Lori and I do our best to adhere to this way of life; so, when the Lord gave me the instruction to write the book I'd been afraid to write, He did so in a very public manner and in a way that I knew it was Him.

The book He was referring to was and is the book you are now reading. Ok, for this to fully resonate with your heart, I need to pivot for a minute and share something with you that happened on Sunday morning, September 8th, 2019.

Throughout all of these decades of our ministry, the Lord has consistently sent us to minister to teenagers outside of the United States. On Thursday afternoon, September 26, 2019, He sent our ministry's Executive Director and me to South Africa where I had been given the honor of ministering at 14 events over the course of four and a half days. Prior to our departure, however, on Sunday morning, September 8th, 2019 I was in our home church and within minutes of the service beginning, our Pastor asked me to get out of my seat and come to the front of the church. And so, I did.

When I got to the altar, our Pastor began to talk to me. The words she then spoke are what the Lord used to give me both the courage and the direction to write this book. This is what the Holy Spirit spoke to me through our Pastor –

"Come here, Dean. I really wanted to do this privately. Dean, this is a GENESIS season for you. All I know is what the Spirit of the Lord showed me is this last season, you literally said to the Lord, 'This almost killed me.' And the Lord said, 'It was designed to do just that.' I saw you in Chrysalis. It sounds so crazy. The Lord said to tell you that this is 'not a mid-life crisis; it's a mid-life Chrysalis.' There's a transformation coming to you and in that Chrysalis, that caterpillar, it dies. It dies. And it's been dark. And, it's been a private pain. But the Lord is about to pour His glory out on you publicly because the enemy tried to destroy you privately.

This is what I heard the Lord say (don't get mad at me). He said, 'I'm about to mess Dean up, really good.' In fact, I saw Jesus laughing as He was messing up your hair. Because He is touching a deep place in you; and the deeper He touches in you, the deeper the river of prophecy will flow through your life. I saw that you were, I wish I could show it. I saw a wavelength of ministry and I saw you go about six feet deeper in that wavelength. There's a deep well the Lord's pulling you from.

The language of your heart is seedtime and harvest and the Lord told me to tell you, 'What has been, that you thought was harvest, was really only the seed for the harvest that's coming.' And I heard the Lord say, 'The blessing He just gave you was not just to make your life easier; it was to make it easier because He's about to put a higher demand; only this demand is an international demand. I hear the Lord saying, 'There are nations calling your name.' He's messing up your hair because some of these places - I hear Lori's voice laughing when the Lord sends you there. But I see a generation of young people who speak other languages there in other places; but the message, YOU MATTER must be heard because they matter. I see that message being written in other languages on tee shirts. YOU MATTER. But the Father told me to remind you, Dean, that you matter. YOU MATTER. YOU MATTER. And He has bottled every tear, He has seen your private struggle, and He says, 'Well done, good and faithful servant.' I see a big check mark on a test paper.

It's an upgrade. It's an upgrade day. It's an upgrade day, Dean. It's an upgrade day, Dean. Somebody just anoint his head with oil. He anoints you from the head down. Your eyes will see differently. Your ears will hear differently; therefore, your mouth will speak differently. There's a metamorphosis happening over

106

your message. Over the revelation the Father is about to give you. And there's international influence coming to you. Can you stretch your hands this way? In the name of Jesus. In the name of Jesus. I'm so sorry, Dean. **There's a book. There's a book from this deep place. I publicly commission you to write from that deep place; write from that deep place and it will bring healing everywhere it goes. This is the book you've been afraid to write, but the Holy Spirit is going to anoint you and anoint your pen to write words that will bring shalom; wholeness to men. Wholeness to God's sons. 'Write it,' says the Lord.**"

As I walked back to my seat that Sunday morning, I did so knowing that the Spirit of God had just spoken to me in such a deep, deep place in my heart. Not only had He just let me know that He intimately knew about the pain in my heart which I had daily lived with for so many years, He also had an assignment that would be helpful in the eradication of this pain – I was to write a new book.

Writing a book was nothing new to our ministry. On average, I've written a new book every year since 1993. What was *new* about this book was the **subject** matter I had been instructed to write about: the subject that *I wasn't enough*. Additionally, there was a **specific time** I was to write this book, and it was imperative that I write it when He told me to write. Not one day earlier.

And so, beginning that Sunday in September, I waited on the Lord. My responsibility was to take what had just been spoken into my life, pray over it, get deeper into the Word of God with it, and to then take time to listen for the still, small voice of God to speak to my heart.

Do you remember that in the early pages of this book I shared with you from the first day I sat down and began journaling, *hurry* had to be eradicated from what the Lord had called me to do? My mind wanted to hurry because of what He had spoken to me through our Pastor on that Sunday morning, but with Lori's consistent encouragement to wait on the Lord and not rush, my

Spirit (my heart) knew that if I hurried the process, I would miss in totality what God wanted to do in my own life. We'd then miss out on the ultimate mission of this book. It's so important to do things God's way and in His timing; otherwise, the alternative is our way and in our timing, aka self-reliance, and self-reliance my friend is part of the curse and the exact opposite of the BLESSING which comes with the GRACE LIFE He's made available to you and me.

Before going any further, I want to share with you one more bit of information that may prove to be very applicable to you and your life moving forward. It's a revelation the Lord gave me as I dove deeper into the emotional and then spiritual realms of my life. Here's some of what happened.

Lori and I were walking together on a beach that we love to visit. As we were walking, our conversation was strained; and as a result, I could feel an internal, emotional volcano quickly rising towards an eruption in my heart. I was about to lose it. Our conversation was strained in large part because the night before, on this same beach, under a moonlit night with the ocean waves crashing behind us, Lori and I had gotten into a disagreement that centered upon me being fully aware of me; me not looking at what Lori was or was not doing, but instead, me keeping the focus on me. (Remember that The Doctor had encouraged me to keep the focus on me and to trust Lori to keep the focus on her.) On this particular night I totally missed it as I chose to focus on Lori and not on me, and that was wrong.

Although I did not disagree with what Lori was saying, I did not want to accept her observations. Just like the waves that were washing onto the shoreline that night, the truth she was sharing was pounding against my heart, a heart that was still coming to terms with and the results of the generational curse of *I wasn't enough*. That conversation did not end well, and so as Lori and I went on a walk together that next morning, we picked up right where we had left off the night before.

It was on this walk that I hit a breaking point and in an instant, I broke. Standing there on that beach as the early morning sun was rising, so many emotions were colliding in my heart and then, when I felt like I could handle no more of these colliding emotions, I broke down and cried. You know, at some point each of us will hit a breaking point and in that moment, how we choose to respond will determine what happens next.

Lori's response was once again one of graciousness. She walked over to me as I stood in the waters of the ocean with tears stinging my eyes; and with compassion that only my wife could have offered in that moment, she lovingly talked with me and then she gave me some space.

As I watched Lori walk off the beach, a song that I had had in my heart weeks earlier came rushing to my heart and mind. Contained within the words of this song is the revelation that I referenced above. This revelation, when applied, can be the turning point that catapults you and me into the greatest and most meaningful seasons of our life. The revelation? I SURRENDER ALL. And our surrendering to His plans and purposes is what this journey of faith is really all about … isn't it? On the day that we surrender, change begins.

A few days after that breaking point on the beach, I had another encounter with Jesus that lasted eight consecutive hours. Those hours felt like only minutes and they were glorious. As His presence saturated the room I was in, His joy captured my heart. Keep in mind what we're taught in Psalm 16:11 – *"You will show me the path of life; in Your PRESENCE is fullness of JOY; at Your right hand are pleasures forevermore."* Did you see it? In the presence of the Lord is the fullness of joy. I had just experienced eight uninterrupted hours of being in His presence. The result? Joy flooded my soul.

With this joy so clearly evident in my heart, I remember looking up to heaven and saying, "Father, from this moment on and for the remainder of my life, I'm asking You to help me as I surrender all of me to all of You. I believe that right here, right now, my heart is healed, and the generational curse is forever gone from my life and the life of our children, in Jesus' name. Father, in the name of Jesus, I ask You to forgive me for my part in the pain I caused my mom and Jesus, I want You to know that I forgive her. Father, I surrender wholly and completely to Your will, in every area of my life … spiritually, physically, emotionally and financially. From this day forward and for the reminder of my life, help me to love Lori the way that she deserves to be loved, the way You want me to love her. Help me Holy Spirit to model to our kids in both my words and in my actions that You have healed my heart and that my life is no longer about me. It's all about You. And because You are the Healer, I believe that You've given me a new heart and a new Spirit. And Sir, I'm so thankful. Father, You've called Lori and me and our family to reach more people for you than ever before in the life of our ministry. I'm now ready to run and finish my race and submit our doing so to You in Your way and in Your timing, in Jesus' name."

As soon as those words left my mouth, instantly the Lord spoke right back to me and said, "I hear you, Dean and I believe you. I've so been looking forward to this moment. I've been with you every step of the way. My heart has yearned for you to allow Me to step in, to reach down, and to touch you with My healing power. As you know, I cannot violate My Word, and so I've been waiting for you to come to the end of yourself. This journey has been painful for you to live but you want to know something, son? It's been painful for Me to watch you go through it. You have no idea in totality all that I have planned for you and Lori and the ministry I've given you. But now, you are ready. Eye has not seen, ear has not heard, nor has entered into your heart all that I have planned for you. Get ready, son. My best for you and Lori, for your family, and for your ministry is here, now. Move out into deeper faith, become more of an intentional worshipper, and watch Me perform My Word in and through your life."

And with all of what I just shared with you about the conversation the Lord and I had, let's make this personal for you and your life. If you are going to walk free from generational curses and the pain that always accompany them, a big part of your doing so will be initiated when you make the choice to embrace true intimacy with Jesus by first surrendering your will to His. Intimacy is defined as a close familiarity or friendship; closeness. What an invitation Jesus is giving you and me to have true intimacy with Him, to have close friendship, closeness, with the One who actually died for you and for me. Sure, at first, intimacy can be very awkward and terribly uncomfortable; but, as we move closer and closer to our Heavenly Father and do so with focused faith and intentionality, the truth of His Word in James 4:8 will show up in our life because, as we *"Draw near to God He will draw near to you."* It's a promise.

Surrender is such a big deal in this journey we know as life. With all of its twists and turns, ups and downs, and victories and defeats, life on our own terms and lived with an attitude of self-reliance, will be challenging at best and disastrous at worst. But to surrender and to do so as an act of your will, now that's a life God can and will use.

Growing up in our church we sang a hymn that maybe you, too, are familiar with. It's a song entitled, *I SURRENDER ALL*, and as you read the words to this song, I encourage you to consider making them the faith anthem that most marks your own life.

All to Jesus I surrender,
All to Him I freely give;
I will ever love and trust Him,
In His presence daily live.
I surrender all,
I surrender all;
All to Thee, my blessed Savior,
I surrender all.
All to Jesus I surrender,
Humbly at His feet I bow;
Worldly pleasures all forsaken,
Take me, Jesus, take me now.
All to Jesus I surrender,
Make me, Savior, wholly Thine;
Let me feel the Holy Spirit,
Truly know that Thou art mine.
All to Jesus I surrender,
Lord, I give myself to Thee;
Fill me with Thy love and power,
Let Thy blessing fall on me.
All to Jesus I surrender,
Now I feel the sacred flame;
Oh, the joy of full salvation!
Glory, glory, to His Name!

These days as I purposefully and consistently take time to inventory my life and the priorities the Lord gives Lori and me to pursue and do so in light of the words of *I SURRENDER ALL*, the cry of my heart is to live this life in a way that causes my Heavenly Father to one-day look at me, smile, and say, "Well done."

And speaking of hearing the words, *"Well done,"* you, too, will one day have that same opportunity, the opportunity to stand before Jesus. Before you do, however, you first have the opportunity to make the choice of a lifetime.

PART FIVE

THE APPLICATION TO YOUR LIFE

THE CHOICE OF A LIFETIME

When speaking in assemblies I almost always connect with students the most when I share with them that God spoke to me and said, "Call Mom", and when I talk with teens about how their choices create circumstances. And right here, right now, I want to talk with you about something that since January of 1993 we have called, *the choice of a lifetime*. We certainly believe that all of what has been shared in the pages of this book is vitally important to you and to your life. This notwithstanding, nothing is more important than offering you the opportunity to make a choice about your relationship with Jesus. I am in no way talking about religion. Much to the contrary, this is 100% about an intimate relationship with a real person who is Love. Jesus is the key to the BLESSING; He and He alone destroyed the curse; and He is the GRACE LIFE.

Let me offer you something that a gentleman by the name of Billy Graham once shared as he was being honored at a luncheon for his lifetime of ministry.

After wonderful things were said about him, Dr. Graham stepped to the rostrum, looked at the crowd, and said, "I'm reminded today of Albert Einstein, the great physicist who this month has been honored by Time magazine as the Man of the Century. Einstein was once traveling from Princeton on a train when the conductor came down the aisle, punching the tickets of every passenger. When he came to Einstein, Einstein reached in his vest pocket. He couldn't find his ticket, so he reached in his trouser pockets. It wasn't there, so he looked in his briefcase but couldn't find it. Then he looked in the seat beside him. He still couldn't find it. The conductor said, "Dr. Einstein, I know who you are. We all know who you are. I'm sure you bought a ticket. Don't worry about it." Einstein nodded appreciatively. The conductor continued down the aisle punching tickets. As he was ready to move to the next car, he turned around and saw the great physicist down on his hands and knees looking under his seat for his ticket. The conductor rushed back and said, "Dr. Einstein, Dr. Einstein, don't worry, I know who you are. No problem. You don't need a ticket. I'm sure you bought one."

Einstein looked at him and said, "Young man, I too, know who I am. What I don't know is *where I'm going.*'"

Having said that Billy Graham continued, "See the suit I'm wearing? It's a brand -new suit. My wife, my children, and my grandchildren are telling me I've gotten a little slovenly in my old age. I used to be a bit more fastidious. So, I went out and bought a new suit for this luncheon and one more occasion.

You know what that occasion is? This is the suit in which I'll be buried. But when you hear I'm dead, I don't want you to immediately remember the suit I'm wearing. I want you to remember this: I not only know who I am ... I also know where I'm going."

May your troubles be less, your blessings more, and may nothing but happiness come through your door."

Isn't that an amazing story? Every time I read about Dr. Einstein on that train, I think about all of the people the Lord allows us to invite to make this very, very personal *choice of a lifetime.* And today, Lori and I hope and pray that by the time you finish reading these next few lines, if you have not yet done so, in a few seconds you, too, will have made this choice. You will then know where you're going; because my friend, Heaven is real, and Jesus is the door through which all of us must walk if Heaven is where you choose to live throughout eternity.

And so, if you're ready to begin this relationship or maybe pick it up where you left it some time ago, I invite you to pray this prayer out loud.

Heavenly Father, I come to You today in faith and in the name of Jesus, believing that You hear my words and that You are ready right now to come live in my heart. And so, according to your Word in Romans 10:9, I declare what Your Word promises: *"That if I confess with my mouth the Lord Jesus and believe in my heart that God has raised Him from the dead, I will be saved."* And so, right here, right now, I believe that Jesus died for me and that He went to hell so that I wouldn't have to. I believe that God raised Jesus from the dead; and today, Jesus, I believe You are seated at the right hand of the Father, talking with Him about me. Jesus, come live in my heart. Be my Lord and my Savior. I surrender to You, in Jesus' name.

If you just prayed that prayer, all of heaven just broke out into a celebration that YOU are now a child of God. And because you are, in Him the curse is destroyed and, you are accepted.

IN HIM, YOU ARE ACCEPTED

As we come to our final minutes together in the pages of this book, my trust is that you are perhaps more hopeful and maybe even more informed about your life than you were when we began our time together. I hope that in my words you have heard my heart. It's a heart that is no longer striving to do something or be anyone other than who He created and invited me to be. It's a heartbeat that so wants to beat in rhythm with the God of heaven and is one that is void of the *fantasy world* that for so very long was such a damaging part of my life. It's a heart that has been healed and sealed with a love that is both allowed in and freely given.

And finally, it's a heart that is just so grateful to be part of the accepted.

In all that the Holy Spirit led me to journal and then in all of the months of writing this book, somewhere in all of these words, in all of the processing, in all of the tears, somewhere, somehow, I once again came face-to-face with Jesus. What a journey this has been and today continues to be. It's an expedition of faith that is available to anyone, anywhere, who is ready to courageously take some time to go deep with Him and as you do, refuse to let the fear that comes with the curse eradicate the faith that comes with the BLESSING.

As you move forward in whatever it is that He has planned for your life, my prayer for you is that you do so knowing that you are loved and have within your reach, the profound truth found in the Word of God, the truth that *love never fails*.

Today, I can honestly share with you that the generational curse that operated in the life of my mom and then in me is no longer part of my life and has not passed to Lori's and my children. No longer do I accept as the truth that *I'm not enough.*

Because of Jesus and the power of love that destroyed a generational curse, I'm so thankful to share with you that because of the choice I made to surrender and the journey that accompanied that decision, in Him, I'm **ACCEPTED**.

ABOUT THE AUTHOR

Since January of 1993, Dean Sikes has been on the road, ministering *words of hope* in high schools across America and in nations of the world. To date, he's spoken at over three thousand five hundred schools, sharing the message of hope with millions of teenagers. The connection he has with teens and young people continues to ignite a conversation encompassing this truth: you matter. And because you matter, you were created to fulfill a purpose and your life has meaning.

Dean is simply a vessel who conveys this truth wholeheartedly to those he encounters. Together with his wife, Lori, the Sikes family make their home in Chattanooga, Tennessee.

DEAN SIKES
POST OFFICE BOX 8915
CHATTANOOGA, TENNESSEE 37414
THE UNITED STATES OF AMERICA

www.deansikes.net